Achieving QTS

Primary Mathematics: Knowledge and Understanding

Second edition

Claire Mooney
Lindsey Ferrie
Sue Fox
Alice Hansen
Reg Wrathmell

Learning Matters

First published in 2000 by Learning Matters Ltd.
Reprinted in 2001.
Second edition published in 2002.
Reprinted in 2002.
Reprinted in 2003.
Reprinted in 2004 (twice).
Reprinted in 2005.
Reprinted in 2006 (twice).

British Library Cataloguing in Publication Data
A CIP record for this book is available from the British Library.

ISBN-13: 978 1 903300 55 8
ISBN-10: 1 903300 55 X

Cover design by Topics – The Creative Partnership
Text design by Code 5 Design Associates Ltd
Project management by Deer Park Productions
Typeset and illustrated by PDQ Typesetting
Printed and bound in Great Britain by Bell & Bain Ltd, Glasgow

Learning Matters Ltd
33 Southernhay East
Exeter EX1 1NX
Tel: 01392 215560
Email: info@learningmatters.co.uk
www.learningmatters.co.uk

CONTENTS

About this book

This book has been written to cater for the needs of primary trainees on all courses of initial teacher training in England and other parts of the UK. By the end of the course, trainees will be required to demonstrate their subject knowledge and understanding and their competence in using this knowledge in their teaching. A secure subject knowledge of mathematics is required for the award of Qualified Teacher Status (QTS) or its equivalent. This book will also be useful to Newly Qualified Teachers (NQTs) and other professionals working in education who have identified aspects of their mathematics subject knowledge which require attention.

This book has been written with the TTA document *Qualifying to Teach: Professional Standards for the Award of Qualified Teacher Status* (2002) firmly at its core. This document clearly states that trainees should have 'a secure knowledge and understanding of the subjects they are trained to teach' (para 2.1). This book aims to address the requirements for trainees' subject knowledge.

Features of this book include:

- **clear links with the Mathematics National Curriculum for England (DfEE/QCA, 1999), the National Numeracy Strategy's (NNS)** *Framework for Teaching Mathematics* **(DfEE, 1999) and the Early Learning Goals (QCA, 1999);**
- **mathematics knowledge and understanding;**
- **research summaries;**
- **practical tasks;**
- **self-assessment questions;**
- **further reading;**
- **glossary.**

This book is structured to ensure clear cross-referencing within and between the chapters. The chapters each have a similar format, with examples that are firmly rooted within a classroom context. There are summaries of each of the chapters, followed by self-assessment questions to further support your subject knowledge development. Answers to all the questions can be found at the end of the book, together with a comprehensive glossary of the mathematical vocabulary developed throughout the chapters.

The chapters are structured in order to link the identified subject knowledge to areas of those documents used to underpin the delivery of mathematics in primary schools. Children's misconceptions are identified within the chapters and the subject knowledge needed by the teacher to effectively support and extend the learning of the child is discussed. This book identifies that which trainees need to know to be able to support children. To address the issues of how to teach children in each of these areas you may want to refer to the accompanying *Primary Mathematics: Teaching Theory and Practice* (Learning Matters, 2000) book.

The chapters

The Number chapter addresses the structural laws underpinning arithmetic. It outlines a range of algorithms for tackling the four rules of number, then extends these into consideration of fractions, decimals and percentages. The concepts of forming equalities and inequalities, of identifying rational and irrational numbers and of representing numbers using index form and standard form are all discussed.

The Algebra chapter deals with identifying and expressing patterns and with the manipulation of symbols, in order to find general terms and solve equations. It addresses the graphical representation of equations and the interpretation of equations, functions and graphs.

The chapter on Measures covers six topics. These are mass/weight, volume/capacity, time, length, surface area and angles. Each of these topics has a section devoted to the subject knowledge. There are a number of practical activities to do in order to experience concepts first hand.

The Shape and Space chapter looks at the systematic naming of 2-D and 3-D shapes. It identifies the properties of these shapes and tackles the transformation of shape. Pythagoras' Theorem is explained as a useful aid and the use of Pi is addressed in the 'circles' section, which also provides information on arcs and sectors. Area is addressed specifically, but surface area and volume are highlighted as a topic in the Measures chapter, although it would be quite feasible to find them in the Shape and Space chapter. As well as concentrating on shapes and transformations, the chapter realises the importance of having the ability to express where in space something is located and as such provides you with detailed information relating to Cartesian Co-ordinates in both one and four quadrants.

The Statistics and Probability chapter outlines the knowledge and skills needed to collect, organise, represent and interpret data. It also addresses issues associated with probability. Having sufficient knowledge of these areas of mathematics will allow confident teaching of handling data to Key Stages 1 and 2. It will also improve the ability to handle data encountered within everyday teaching.

The Mathematical Language, Reasoning and Proof chapter tackles two issues. In one way it can be read as an extension chapter considering the ideas of proof within mathematics. Having gained all the other knowledge, how can this be used to prove beyond doubt that something is true? The idea of using mathematical knowledge to develop rigorous argument also addresses this area. The other aspect of this chapter, that of mathematical language, touches on every area of mathematics. The importance of developing a precise mathematical vocabulary is emphasised and some of the issues associated with social usage of language are considered.

A subject knowledge of mathematics really does matter!

A healthy subject knowledge of mathematics is widely acknowledged as a critical factor in the complex process of teaching mathematics itself. Few nowadays would argue that planning, teaching and assessing mathematics lessons, setting learning outcomes, choosing appropriate activities and resources, identifying children's errors and misconceptions, asking and responding to questions, and so on, could be achieved without a sound knowledge of mathematics in the first place. Within primary schools currently there is a clear drive to raise standards in mathematics through raising expectations and national target-setting. The NNS *Framework* supports the development of a coherent and progressive mathematics curriculum within schools. However, implicit within this drive to raise standards in mathematics is the requirement for teachers to have the necessary subject knowledge to teach confidently and effectively; motivating, challenging and extending the children.

The Professional Standards for QTS

The Professional Standards for QTS, found in *Qualifying to Teach* (TTA, 2002) are presented in three interrelated secions. Section 1 identifies professional values and practice; section 2 the knowledge and understanding required by teachers; section 3 the skills related to teaching. This book is written to support the development of trainees' subject knowledge and understanding of mathematics as required in section 2.

In order to support the development of a secure knowledge and understanding of mathematics, this book addresses the following areas:

* **the real number system;**
* **indices;**
* **number operations and algebra;**
* **equations, functions and graphs;**
* **mathematical reasoning and proof;**
* **measures;**
* **shape and space;**
* **probability and statistics.**

Mathematics in the National Curriculum

Mathematics in the National Curriculum is organised on the basis of four Key Stages. Key Stage 1 for 5- to 7-year-olds (Years 1 and 2) and Key Stage 2 for 7- to 11-year-olds (Years 3 to 6) are for primary. The components of each Key Stage include Programmes of Study, which set out the mathematics that children should be taught; Attainment

Targets, which set out the mathematical knowledge, skills and understanding that children should attain; and Level Descriptions, which describe the types and range of performance that children working at a particular level should be able to demonstrate within each Attainment Target. Mathematics in the National Curriculum is a minimum statutory requirement. Since its introduction in 1989 it has been significantly revised three times. The Programmes of Study for mathematics currently include:

- **Ma 1: Using and Applying Mathematics;**
- **Ma 2: Number and Algebra;**
- **Ma 3: Shape, Space and Measures;**
- **Ma 4: Handling Data.**

Mathematics in the National Curriculum also presents links to other subjects, and suggestions for the use of ICT.

National Numeracy Strategy – *Framework for Teaching Mathematics*

The NNS *Framework for Teaching Mathematics* is a non-statutory document. With the arrival of the revised Mathematics National Curriculum for England (DfEE/QCA, 1999), however, it can be seen that the two documents mirror each other extremely closely. The *Framework* is intended to supplement the NC Order and offer a sort of national 'scheme of work' for mathematics. It identifies certain 'key objectives' for each year group and encourages recording attainment against these. It also clearly details far more teaching objectives within the yearly teaching programmes. These should be used to support termly planning. The *Framework* is designed to be used flexibly both for the planning and the teaching of mathematics.

Curriculum Guidance for the Foundation Stage

The Curriculum Guidance for the Foundation Stage details that which most children should achieve by the end of their reception year. It identifies features of good practice during the Foundation Stage (the Foundation Stage begins when children reach the age of three) and sets out the early learning goals within the context of six areas. One of these areas is that of mathematical development. The early learning goals for mathematical development mirror exactly the NNS key objectives for reception.

Outcomes

This book can be used to start to address the development of mathematical subject knowledge. But more broadly than that, through developing subject knowledge of mathematics including patterns and relationships, the ability to communicate, discuss, generalise, hypothesise and relate mathematics to the wider world, more positive and active attitudes towards and greater enthusiasm for mathematics will be developed. It should also stimulate a sense of curiosity and enjoyment and encourage communication of these positive attitudes to the children, resulting in teaching that is effective, challenging and extremely rewarding.

Statutory and exemplary documentation

DfEE/QCA (1999) *Mathematics: the National Curriculum for England.* London: HMSO.

DfEE (1999) *The National Numeracy Strategy: Framework for Teaching Mathematics.* London: DfEE.

QCA (2000) *Curriculum Guidance for the Foundation Stage.* London: QCA.

TTA (2002) *Qualifying to Teach: Professional Standards for the Award of Qualified Teacher Status and Requirements for Initial Teacher Training.* London: TTA.

2 NUMBER

Introduction

For thousands of years people have used numbers to keep records, to investigate, to solve problems and to predict. These uses often had very concrete applications; for example, recording crop yields at harvest. As the use of number became more complex, formal operations were used. These form the basis of arithmetic (from the Greek *arithmetike* – the art of numbers). When Pythagoras (582–507 BCE) founded the Pythagorean Brotherhood it became, in effect, a religious community and one of the things it worshipped was Number. From the ancient Egyptians, the Greeks and the Babylonians to the present day, number has formed an intrinsic part of daily life. Spend 24 hours noting all the times you encounter numbers in any context and you will be truly amazed at just how numerate we need to be to function effectively within society today.

 For more information on the Pythagorean Brotherhood, see page 80 for the section on Pythagoras' Theorem.

Professional Standards for QTS

→ 2.1b

To achieve QTS you need to have a secure knowledge and understanding of the mathematics content of the National Curriculum for Key Stages 1 and 2 and the methods and expectations set out in the National Numeracy Strategy. For Number this includes:

- *The real number system:*
  - *the arithmetic of integers, fractions and decimals;*
  - *forming equalities and inequalities and recognising when equality is preserved;*
  - *the distinction between a rational number and an irrational number; making sense of simple recurring decimals.*
- *Indices:*
  - *representing numbers in index form including positive and negative integer exponents;*
  - *standard form.*
- *Number operations and algebra:*
  - *using the associative, commutative and distributive laws;*
  - *use of cancellation to simplify calculations;*
  - *using the multiplicative structure of ratio and proportion to solve problems;*
  - *finding factors and multiples of numbers and of simple algebraic expressions.*

You may find it helpful to read through the appropriate section of the Handbook that accompanies the Standards for the award of QTS for clarification and support.

Curriculum Guidance for the Foundation Stage, the National Curriculum and the National Numeracy Strategy

The Curriculum Guidance for the Foundation Stage recognises the importance of certain key skills in mathematical development. The areas identified include counting and working with numbers. The mathematical understanding of the children should be developed through games, songs, stories and play to encourage experimenting with numbers, including those larger than 10.

Within the Mathematics National Curriculum, the Number Programmes of Study state the knowledge, skills and understanding which are to be taught throughout Key Stages 1 and 2. These are closely linked to the Key Objectives identified for each year group within the NNS *Framework for Teaching Mathematics*.

At Key Stage 1, children should be taught about numbers and the number system through counting and number patterns and sequences. They start to calculate, both mentally and on paper, by developing an understanding of number operations and relationships. They use this understanding to solve numerical problems.

During Key Stage 2, children further develop their understanding of these concepts. They start to explore positive and negative integers, fractions, decimals and percentages, ratio and more challenging patterns and sequences. They increase their range of mental calculation strategies and move towards standard written algorithms.

RESEARCH SUMMARY

Eddie Gray's research has distinguished between the processes in mathematics and the procedures. He believes that processes do not include any implication that they are carried out in a unique manner. For example, the 'process of addition' might use counting on or a formal written algorithm, but which method is not implied in the process. Conversely 'procedure' describes a specific algorithm. Children who interpret processes only as procedures make mathematics harder for themselves. Children who do not restrict their understanding of processes to procedures, see processes as flexible procepts. The divergence between the two he refers to as the 'proceptual divide'. He argues that the difference between success and failure lies in the difference between the use of procepts and procedures.

Julia Anghileri stresses the importance of understanding appropriate language prior to tackling multiplication and division. This was revealed in research using sticks made up of differently coloured cubes. For example, using sticks 8 cubes long, with 2 cubes of each colour, the children were asked to identify how many colours there were. For many of the children the 'how many' led them to count all, i.e. 8. They were then asked to make a pattern stick using 5 different colours with 3 of each colour. A common error was producing a stick with 5 cubes of different colours and 3 further cubes. There was a difficulty in identifying the roles of the numbers 3 and 5 and also of the term 'each'. 'Each' is fundamentally important to understanding multiplication and division.

Nunes and Bryant (1996) cite Campos et al. (1995) who found that introducing children to fractions as shapes divided into equal units with some coloured can lead children into errors. They claim that pupils employ a 'double counting procedure' by counting the total parts for the denominator and the shaded parts for the numerator without real understanding of the concept of fractions.

PrIME (Primary Initiative in Mathematics Education) (1985–89) found that through experimentation with a calculator, children in infant classes were familiar with negative numbers. Keying in 5 − 9 would give the result −4. Similarly experimenting with number patterns can result in the child working with negative numbers. Repeated subtraction of 3 starting with 10: 10, 7, 4, 1, −2, −5, −8 and so on.

The *Framework for Teaching Mathematics* provides detailed objectives for planning and teaching these areas of mathematics. In common with the National Curriculum, it emphasises developing a clear understanding of the number system and properties of number, together with efficient and effective mental and written calculation strategies.

Knowledge and understanding

Before considering any children's misconceptions with number or the subject knowledge you will need to support them, there are certain fundamental laws which underpin all work in arithmetic. It is important that you have a very clear understanding of these before considering other aspects.

Precedence – BODMAS

Before considering the laws governing the operations it is important to understand that precedence is given to particular operations when working out a complex expression. For example, how would you solve:

$$8 - 3 \times (4 + 2) + 16 \div 4 - 2 \times 3$$

If the expression is attempted simply working left to right, the answer obtained would be:

$$8 - 3 = 5, \text{ then} \times 6 \text{ (i.e. } 4 + 2) = 30, \text{ next} + 16 = 46,$$
$$\text{now} \div 4 = 11.5, \text{ then} -2 = 9.5, \text{ finally} \times 3 = 28.5$$

This is incorrect, however, due to mathematical convention which gives a specific order for tackling such problems. The order can be summarised as BODMAS. BODMAS stands for:

B – brackets
O – of
D – division
M– multiplication
A – addition
S – subtraction

When solving expressions such as the one above, convention dictates that the brackets are solved first, followed by any 'of', division and multiplication operations, finally addition and subtraction are considered. For the above example this gives:

$$
\begin{aligned}
& 8 - 3 \times (4 + 2) + 16 \div 4 - 2 \times 3 \\
={} & 8 - 3 \times \quad 6 \quad + 16 \div 4 - 2 \times 3 \quad \text{(tackling brackets first)} \\
={} & 8 - \quad 18 \quad\quad + \quad 4 \quad - \quad 6 \quad\quad \text{(now working out the} \times \text{and} \div) \\
={} & -12 \quad\quad\quad\quad\quad\quad\quad\quad\quad\quad\quad \text{(finally completing the} + \text{and} -)
\end{aligned}
$$

Try the following example before looking at the workings shown:

$$3 + 4 \times (3 - 1) + 6 \div 3 - 5$$

Applying the BODMAS order of precedence gives:

$$
\begin{aligned}
&\ \ 3 + 4 \times (3 - 1)\ \ + 6 \div 3\ \ - 5 \\
&= \ 3 + \ \ \ 4 \times 2\ \ \ \ \ \ + 6 \div 3\ \ - 5 \qquad \text{(brackets first)} \\
&= \ 3 + \ \ \ \ \ 8\ \ \ \ \ \ \ \ \ + \ \ 2\ \ \ \ - 5 \qquad \text{(now} \times \text{and} \div) \\
&= \ 8 \qquad\qquad\qquad\qquad\qquad\qquad \text{(finally} + \text{and} -)
\end{aligned}
$$

Laws of arithmetic

Having considered the order of precedence of the operations, it is necessary to understand the structural laws which apply. There are three laws of arithmetic that underpin calculations using the four operations. These laws are:

- *the commutative law;*
- *the associative law;*
- *the distributive law.*

THE COMMUTATIVE LAW

This law basically states that the order in which the operation is performed makes no difference to the answer. For which of the four rules (addition, subtraction, multiplication and division) does this hold true? Using some numerical examples it can be seen that addition gives:

$$6 + 3 = 3 + 6$$

Subtraction:

$$6 - 3 \neq 3 - 6$$

Multiplication:

$$6 \times 3 = 3 \times 6$$

Division:

$$6 \div 3 \neq 3 \div 6$$

Generally the operations of addition and multiplication are commutative for any numbers a and b:

$$a + b = b + a \qquad\qquad a \times b = b \times a$$

THE ASSOCIATIVE LAW

This law means that numbers can be regrouped to simplify a question while making no difference to the answer. The fact that numbers can be grouped and combined in different ways is very helpful during certain calculations where a reordering of the component numbers will ease the difficulty of the calculation. This is essential for the development of appropriate mental calculation strategies. For which of the four rules does this hold true? Using some numerical examples it can be seen that addition gives:

$$(2 + 3) + 7 = 2 + (3 + 7)$$

Subtraction:

$$(10 - 2) - 1 \neq 10 - (2 - 1)$$

Multiplication:

$$(2 \times 3) \times 7 = 2 \times (3 \times 7)$$

Division:

$$(12 \div 6) \div 2 \neq 12 \div (6 \div 2)$$

Generally the operations of addition and multiplication are associative for any numbers a, b and c:

$$(a + b) + c = a + (b + c) \qquad (a \times b) \times c = a \times (b \times c)$$

THE DISTRIBUTIVE LAW

The distributive law is so called as it involves one operation being 'distributed out' over another operation. A simple example of this law is to answer the following problem mentally. You go into a shop and buy five pairs of socks costing £4.99 a pair. How much do you spend?

The obvious way to answer this is to say, 'That's 5×£5 take away 5p which gives £24.95.' How can this be written down?

$$5 \times (£5 - 1p) = (5 \times £5) - (5 \times 1p)$$

Because £4.99 = £5 − 1p

Generally this distributive law of multiplication *over* subtraction can be written:

$$a \times (b - c) = (a \times b) - (a \times c)$$

This also holds true for multiplication over addition:

$$a \times (b + c) = (a \times b) + (a \times c)$$

But does it hold true for division over addition and subtraction? This is a very interesting question. Consider the following example for multiplication over addition:

$$2 \times (3 + 4) = (2 \times 3) + (2 \times 4)$$

Due to the commutative law, this would give exactly the same answer if it was written:

$$(3 + 4) \times 2 = (3 \times 2) + (4 \times 2)$$

Next consider the following numerical example for division over addition:

$$2 \div (4 + 6) \neq (2 \div 4) + (2 \div 6)$$

However,

$$(4 + 6) \div 2 = (4 \div 2) + (6 \div 2)$$

Because of this, division is said to be *right* distributive over addition and subtraction.

This means that as long as the **dividend** (number being divided) is the number that is 'split' the law holds. However, if it is the **divisor** (the number dividing into the dividend) which is split, then the law does not hold. Put more crudely, the division needs to be on the right side of the brackets, hence right distributive.

Expressed generally: $a \div (b + c) \neq (a \div b) + (a \div c)$

however: $(a + b) \div c = (a \div c) + (b \div c)$

and also: $(a - b) \div c = (a \div c) - (b \div c)$

Having considered the laws underpinning calculations, this chapter will now identify some misconceptions which you might encounter in the classroom. The appropriate subject knowledge you will need to support the children's learning will be discussed.

Calculation

Think about this

Ayesha is asked to add the following numbers:

  25, 175, 50, 200, 5

She tackles the problem as follows:

        25
        175
    + 50
        200
        5
    ‾‾‾‾‾‾
    1625

What does this tell you about her understanding of addition?

Firstly it is clear that Ayesha does not yet have a sufficient understanding of place value to tackle column addition and should be using a different method. This example really encourages mental calculation. If she wanted to use a written method, an expanded written form would be far more appropriate. What knowledge do you need to be able to effectively support Ayesha to develop a greater understanding of calculation?

Place Value

In order to tackle standard written algorithms it is important to have a very clear understanding of place value. Place value is used by number systems that allow the same digit to carry different values based on its position, i.e. the *place* has a particular *value*. We use the Hindu-Arabic base 10 number system. The ancient Egyptians also used a base 10 system but they did not have a place value concept. The earliest known example of a place value system was that of the Babylonians. They worked in bases 60 and 360. We still use bases 60 and 360 in some areas ourselves, e.g. 360 degrees in a complete turn and 60 seconds in a minute, 60 minutes in an hour.

Our place value number system has certain principles:

- the idea of treating a group of objects as a unit, so ten ones can be one unit of ten and ten tens, one unit of a hundred;
- using the same symbols repeatedly so all numbers can be represented using the 10 digits: 0, 1, 2, 3, 4, 5, 6, 7, 8 and 9;
- the position of the digit relative to any other digits in the number determines its value; the larger groupings are always on the left;
- to identify the size of the number you need to work out the value of each of the digits and then add them, e.g. in 358, the 3 represents 300, the 5 represents 50 and the 8 is 8 ones. The total value of the whole number is the sum of these values, 300 + 50 + 8 = 358.

For more information on Al-Khwarizmi, see page 42 for the section on knowledge and understanding.

The role of 0 as a 'place holder' is crucial. When 2 is multiplied by 10, the answer is 20. There are now 2 tens instead of 2 units. The zero is holding the place for the units to show that the units column is empty. *Zero* comes from the Latin *zephirum*, which means empty or blank. The symbol 0 originated in India. Al-Khwarizmi explained the Indian number system in AD 830, but it took a further 400 years before zero was used in western number systems.

The four rules of number

The four rules of number are **addition**, **subtraction**, **multiplication** and **division**. There are various relationships between these rules. Addition can be viewed as the **inverse** of subtraction and subtraction as the **inverse** of addition. Equally multiplication and division can be seen as inverse operations. Multiplication can be tackled as repeated addition and division as repeated subtraction. There is a range of methods for solving problems involving each of these operations.

Addition

It is important to recognise that many addition problems can be solved quickly and efficiently using mental methods. Many mental strategies involve working left-to-right, i.e. largest columns first. For example, adding 234 and 325 mentally could give rise to the following steps:

'Two hundred add three hundred gives five hundred. Thirty add twenty gives fifty, and four add five is nine. So it is five hundred and fifty nine.'

EXPANDED WRITTEN METHOD

This method allows for an informal pencil and paper calculation, which builds on the mental strategies already discussed.

To tackle a problem such as 324 + 438 it is first necessary to write the question vertically:

```
   324
+  438
   700  (add the hundreds first)
    50  (add the tens next)
    12  (then add the units)
   762  (finally add mentally top to bottom or bottom to top)
```

This method can be used whatever the size of the numbers. For example, 2468 + 1357:

```
   2468
+  1357
   3000
    700
    110
     15
   3825
```

A STANDARD ALGORITHM

The standard written algorithm for addition can be viewed as shorthand notation for this expanded method. Looking at this example again using the standard algorithm gives:

```
   2468
+  1357
   3825
    I I
```

represents the 100 in 60 + 50 = 110   represents the 10 in 8 + 7 = 15

Subtraction

As with addition there are many effective and efficient strategies for tackling subtraction problems mentally. The first example of a written method below draws upon one such example, that of 'counting on' or complementary addition.

COMPLEMENTARY ADDITION

This method builds upon the mental method which frequently involves the visual image of an empty number line. To answer the question 84 − 46, the difference is found by counting on from the smaller to the larger number in steps along the number line:

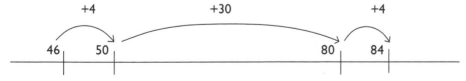

Hence the answer to 84 − 46 is 4 + 30 + 4 which is 38.

This method can be extended in written form giving an informal pencil and paper method for complementary addition. Using the above example gives:

```
        84
      − 46
         4    (to 50)
        30    (to 80)
         4    (to 84)
        38
```

This method can be applied equally effectively to larger numbers. For example, 5356 − 1583:

```
        5356              or       5356
      − 1583                     − 1583
          17    (to 1600)            17
         400    (to 2000)           400
        3356    (to 5356)          3356
        3000                       3773
         700                          I
          60
          13
        3773
```

DECOMPOSITION

This method is the one that is frequently taught as the standard algorithm for subtraction. It involves regrouping numbers to support the calculation. For example, 143 − 27:

	Hundreds	Tens	Units
	1	3	1 3
−		2	7
	1	1	6

Written in the conventional way this gives:

```
       3 1
    1 4̷3
  −   2 7
    1 1 6
```

This method works for any numbers. Looking at the last example given for the complementary addition method, 5356 − 1583, gives:

```
     4 12 1
    5̷3̷5 6
  − 1 5 8 3
    3 7 7 3
```

This method involves keeping the overall value of the **minuend** the same throughout the calculation. The **minuend** is the number from which something is being subtracted. The **subtrahend** is the number subtracted.

EQUAL ADDITION

This method of subtraction involves changing the value of both the minuend and subtrahend by the same amount. It is based on the fact that if the same number is added to both, the difference remains unchanged. This was taught as the 'borrow and pay back' method of subtraction in schools in the earlier parts of the twentieth century.

Looking at the first example in decomposition, $143 - 27$, the equal addition method gives:

$$
\begin{array}{r}
1\,4\,{}^{\scriptstyle 1}3 \\
-\,{}^{\scriptstyle 1}2\,7 \\
\hline
1\,1\,6
\end{array}
$$

10 is added to the minuend

10 is added to the subtrahend to ensure the difference is unchanged

Areas of potential confusion lie in the language of 'borrow', the obvious question being 'where from?' One way of traditionally setting out these questions can also give rise to difficulty. For example, the 10 being added to the units in the minuend is represented in the same way as the 10 being added to the tens column in the subtrahend. However, these tens are treated differently in the calculation. So, $^{1}3$ in the minuend represents 13 units but $^{1}2$ in the subtrahend represents 3 tens and not 12 as suggested by the representation in the minuend.

These potential confusions aside, this method offers an effective way of undertaking these calculations that is closely linked to balancing equations within algebra.

Consider the final example from decomposition, $5356 - 1583$, and try to answer the question using the equal addition method.

$$
\begin{array}{r}
5\,{}^{\scriptstyle 1}3\,{}^{\scriptstyle 1}5\,6 \\
-\,{}^{\scriptstyle 1}1\,{}^{\scriptstyle 1}5\,8\,3 \\
\hline
3\,7\,7\,3
\end{array}
$$

Multiplication

As already seen with addition and subtraction, there is a wide range of strategies that can be used to multiply numbers. This chapter will consider some of the informal written methods, which are frequently derived from mental methods. It will also outline some more standard methods of multiplying using pencil and paper calculations.

REPEATED ADDITION

One of the earliest methods of multiplying involves knowledge of the relationship between addition and multiplication. Once it is realised that multiplication can be seen as repeated addition then this fact can be used to solve simple multiplication problems. For example, 6 × 4:

This can be calculated as 4 + 4 + 4 + 4 + 4 + 4 = 24

It can quickly be seen that this method is rather limited and would be very cumbersome for large calculations. However, knowledge of multiplication by 10, 100, 1000, … can be used along with repeated addition to extend this method. For example, 354 × 232:

$$
\begin{array}{rll}
354 \times 100 &= 35400 \\
354 \times 100 &= 35400 & \text{200} \times 354 \\
354 \times 10 &= 3540 \\
354 \times 10 &= 3540 & \text{30} \times 354 \\
354 \times 10 &= 3540 \\
354 \times 1 &= 354 \\
354 \times 1 &= 354 & \text{2} \times 354 \\
&\ \underline{82128} & \underline{232 \times 354}
\end{array}
$$

A STANDARD ALGORITHM

 For more information on the distributive law see page 10.

The standard algorithm frequently taught is dependent upon the **distributive law**. This means that a question such as 24 × 35 is actually tackled as (24 × 30) + (24 × 5):

$$
\begin{array}{rl}
& 2\ 4 \\
\times & 3\ 5 \\
\hline
& 1\ 2_20 \quad (5 \times 24) \\
& 7_12\ 0 \quad (30 \times 24) \\
\hline
& 8\ 4\ 0 \quad (35 \times 24)
\end{array}
$$

To see what is happening it is possible to write this in an expanded form:

$$
\begin{array}{rl}
& 24 \\
\times & 35 \\
\hline
& 20 \longrightarrow 5 \times 4 \\
& 100 \longrightarrow 5 \times 20 \\
& 120 \longrightarrow 30 \times 4 \\
& \underline{600} \longrightarrow 30 \times 20 \\
& 840 \longrightarrow 35 \times 24
\end{array}
$$

The standard algorithm is a shorthand version of the above form.

A TABULAR METHOD

Another way of tackling multiplication which illustrates how it is underpinned by the distributive law involves a tabular form of calculation. For example, taking the example of 24 × 35 above:

×	30	5	
20	600	100	700
4	120	20	140
			840

This is a very useful method as it makes explicit how the distributive law applies to multiplication.

GELOSIA MULTIPLICATION

This method of multiplication dates back to twelfth-century India. It is also sometimes called 'Chinese' multiplication, 'lattice' multiplication or 'grating' multiplication. This method depends on producing a grid so that place value is implicit within the structure. Take the above example of 35×24:

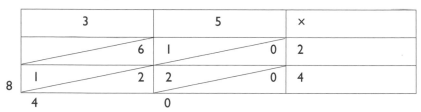

The digits at the top of the grid are multiplied in turn by those down the side. The answers to each of these multiplications are written in the boxes, the tens value being written above the diagonal line and the units value below. Finally the numbers in each diagonal are added, carrying as necessary to the next diagonal.

For more informaiton on Gelosia multiplication, see page 27 for the section on multiplication of decimals.

This method can also be applied to the multiplication of decimals.

Division

As above with the other operations, there is a wide range of strategies that can be used to divide numbers. This section will start by considering informal written methods, which are frequently derived from mental methods. It will also outline some more standard methods of dividing using pencil and paper calculations.

REPEATED SUBTRACTION

One of the earliest methods of dividing involves knowledge of the relationship between subtraction and division. Once it is realised that division can be seen as repeated subtraction then this fact can be used to solve simple division problems. For example, $24 \div 6$:

This can be calculated as
$$24 - 6 = 18$$
$$18 - 6 = 12$$
$$12 - 6 = 6$$
$$6 - 6 = 0 \quad \text{How many times has 6 been subtracted? 4}$$

It can quickly be seen that this method is rather limited and would be very cumbersome for large calculations. However, knowledge of multiplication by 10, 100, 1000, . . . can be used along with repeated subtraction to extend this method. For example, $28875 \div 231$:

$$231 \times 100 = 23100$$

$$\begin{array}{r} 2\,8\,8\,7\,5 \\ -2\,3\,1\,0\,0 \\ \hline 5\,7\,7\,5 \end{array}$$

$$231 \times 10 = 2310$$

$$\begin{array}{r} 5\,7\,7\,5 \\ -2\,3\,1\,0 \\ \hline 3\,4\,6\,5 \end{array}$$

$$231 \times 10 = 2310$$

$$\begin{array}{r} 3\,4\,6\,5 \\ -2\,3\,1\,0 \\ \hline 1\,1\,5\,5 \end{array}$$

$$1155 - 231 = 924$$
$$924 - 231 = 693$$
$$693 - 231 = 462$$
$$462 - 231 = 231$$
$$231 - 231 = 0$$

How many times has 231 been subtracted from 28875? Simply add to find out:

$$100 + 10 + 10 + 1 + 1 + 1 + 1 + 1 = 125$$

TRADITIONAL LONG DIVISION

The traditional method for long division, frequently taught as a standard algorithm, is really a shorthand version of a method not unlike the repeated subtraction method shown above. The traditional algorithm for $7404 \div 6$ is as follows:

$$\begin{array}{r} 1\,2\,3\,4 \\ 6\,)\overline{7\,4\,0\,4} \\ \underline{6} \\ 1\,4 \\ \underline{1\,2} \\ 2\,0 \\ \underline{1\,8} \\ 2\,4 \\ \underline{2\,4} \\ 0 \end{array}$$

(6×1, hence 1 in the thousands column of the answer)

(6×2, hence 2 in the hundreds column of the answer)

(6×3, hence 3 in the tens column of the answer)

(6×4, hence 4 in the units column of the answer)

This should really be viewed as shorthand for the following arrangement if this method is to have any meaning.

$$\begin{array}{r} 1\,2\,3\,4 \\ 6\,)\overline{7\,4\,0\,4} \\ \underline{6\,0\,0\,0} \\ 1\,4\,0\,4 \\ \underline{1\,2\,0\,0} \\ 2\,0\,4 \\ \underline{1\,8\,0} \\ 2\,4 \\ \underline{2\,4} \\ 0 \end{array}$$

(6×1000)

(6×200)

(6×30)

(6×4)

TRADITIONAL LONG DIVISION (ABBREVIATED)

It is possible to attempt the above question using an abbreviated form of long division. Some people are taught this as their standard algorithm. This method is illustrated using the same example, $7404 \div 6$.

$$\begin{array}{r} 1\,2\,3\,4 \\ 6\,\overline{)\,7^1 4^2 0^2 4} \end{array}$$

Here 6 is divided into each of the digits in turn, any remainder is 'carried over' to the next column.

Negative numbers

Integers are positive or negative whole numbers. When considering the four rules of number it is important to consider how they relate to calculations involving negative numbers.

Calculations with negative numbers can be simplified with the use of a number line:

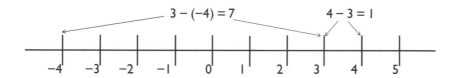

- **4 − 3 can be read as 'find the difference between 4 and 3' with the answer being 1.**
- **Similarly 3 − (−4) can be read as 'find the difference between 3 and −4'. Looking at the number line it is easy to see that there is a difference of seven. This is much more convincing than just remembering that 'two minuses make a plus', thus making 3 − (−4) into 3 + 4 without any understanding.**
- **When adding a negative number, the commutative property of addition can be used. This means that 2 + (−1) = (−1) + 2 and (−1) + 2 = 1.**

Multiplication and division of negative numbers also give rise to certain rules, but how are these rules arrived at?

Above it has been shown how 'two minuses make a plus' but how does this relate to multiplication?

- **Consider the problem 6 × (−6). It is clear that this is 6 lots of −6, which is equal to −36. But what about (−6) × (−6)? This will give the negative, or opposite, of 6 × (−6), so if 6 × (−6) = −36 then (−6) × (−6) must be equal to 36.**
- **This is also true for division. Consider (−36) ÷ (−6). This is one way of writing how many −6s in −36. The answer to this is clearly 6. Therefore when considering 36 ÷ (−6) the answer is the negative, or opposite, of the previous answer i.e. −6.**

As can be seen from all of these algorithms for the four rules, Ayesha needs to start working on non-standard or informal methods before attempting to calculate using formal algorithms.

Fractions

Lotti is asked to add the following fractions, $\frac{1}{4} + \frac{1}{4} + \frac{1}{2}$.
She tackles the problem as follows:

$$\frac{1}{4} + \frac{1}{4} + \frac{1}{2} = \frac{2}{8} + \frac{1}{2} = \frac{3}{10}$$

What does this tell you about her understanding of fractions and addition of fractions?

It is clear that Lotti does not understand that the denominator indicates the number of fractional parts the unit has been divided into, whilst the numerator indicates how many parts of this size there are. An understanding of this is essential if she is to successfully add fractions either mentally or using a pencil and paper method.

$\dfrac{1}{2}$ ⟵   **numerator**

     ⟵   **denominator**

Fractions have formed a useful part of mathematics since ancient Egyptian times. Because they did not a have a place value system, the Egyptians only used unit fractions, e.g. $\frac{1}{2}$, $\frac{1}{3}$, $\frac{1}{9}$, $\frac{1}{24}$ etc., as to attempt anything more complex would have involved extremely cumbersome calculations. Think of the Babylonian system which used base 60. When considering unit fractions, base 60 is very useful, because 60 has so many factors. For example, $\frac{1}{2}$, $\frac{1}{3}$, $\frac{1}{4}$, $\frac{1}{5}$, $\frac{1}{6}$, $\frac{1}{10}$, $\frac{1}{12}$, $\frac{1}{15}$, $\frac{1}{20}$, $\frac{1}{30}$ would all give whole number answers as fractions of an hour. It is important to remember what the notation means; $\frac{1}{2}$ is a form of writing 1 unit divided into 2 parts. Similarly $\frac{5}{3}$ can be read as 5 divided into 3 groups.

The use of fractions falls into two main areas:

- **as a measurement such as $\frac{1}{4}$ hour or $\frac{1}{2}$ kilometre where the fraction is being used to express part of a unit (in this case hours and kilometres);**
- **as an operator on another number, as in $\frac{1}{4}$ of 24.**

Within these areas, there are five different types of fractions:

- **part of a complete unit or 'whole';**

- **a comparison between a subset and a whole set;**

 $\frac{4}{5}$ of the dots are black

- a number, the point on a line between two whole numbers;

- the result of division of whole numbers;

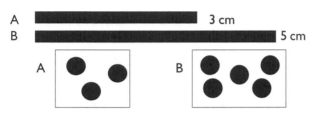

There are 3 bars of chocolate to share equally between 4 people – each person would receive $\frac{3}{4}$ of the total chocolate.

- comparing the sizes of two measurements or two sets of objects.

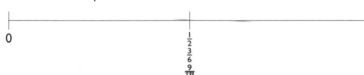

A is $\frac{3}{5}$ as long as B

A has $\frac{3}{5}$ as many as B

 For more information on comparing sizes, see page 36 for the section on ratio and proportion.

EQUIVALENT FRACTIONS

One of the most important concepts in the development of understanding of fractions is that of **equivalence**. Equivalent fractions have the same value and so appear on a number line in the same place.

A useful prompt to help 'see' these 'fraction families' is the fraction wall. The recognition of the numerical pattern of these fractions is also vital. For example:

(a) $\frac{1}{2}, \frac{2}{4}, \frac{4}{8}, \frac{8}{16}$ (b) $\frac{1}{2}, \frac{2}{4}, \frac{3}{6}, \frac{4}{8}$

What would the next equivalent fraction be in each case?

(a) the numerator and the denominator are both being multiplied by 2 to ensure the fractions are equivalent to $\frac{1}{2}$, hence the next fraction in the family would be $\frac{16}{32}$.
(b) the numerator is increasing by 1 each time, the denominator is double the numerator as these fractions are all equivalent to $\frac{1}{2}$. Hence the next fraction in the family would be $\frac{5}{10}$.

One whole							
One half				One half			
One quarter		One quarter		One quarter		One quarter	
$\frac{1}{8}$		$\frac{1}{8}$		$\frac{1}{8}$		$\frac{1}{8}$		$\frac{1}{8}$		$\frac{1}{8}$		$\frac{1}{8}$		$\frac{1}{8}$	
$\frac{1}{16}$	$\frac{1}{16}$	$\frac{1}{16}$	$\frac{1}{16}$	$\frac{1}{16}$	$\frac{1}{16}$	$\frac{1}{16}$	$\frac{1}{16}$	$\frac{1}{16}$	$\frac{1}{16}$	$\frac{1}{16}$	$\frac{1}{16}$	$\frac{1}{16}$	$\frac{1}{16}$	$\frac{1}{16}$	$\frac{1}{16}$

Using the wall it is easy to see that $\frac{1}{2} = \frac{2}{4} = \frac{4}{8}$ and that $\frac{3}{4} = \frac{6}{8}$ and $\frac{1}{4} = \frac{2}{8}$, and so on.

One whole											
One third				One third				One third			
One sixth		One sixth		One sixth		One sixth		One sixth		One sixth	
$\frac{1}{9}$		$\frac{1}{9}$		$\frac{1}{9}$		$\frac{1}{9}$		$\frac{1}{9}$		$\frac{1}{9}$	
$\frac{1}{12}$	$\frac{1}{12}$	$\frac{1}{12}$	$\frac{1}{12}$	$\frac{1}{12}$	$\frac{1}{12}$	$\frac{1}{12}$	$\frac{1}{12}$	$\frac{1}{12}$	$\frac{1}{12}$	$\frac{1}{12}$	$\frac{1}{12}$

Using this wall it can be seen that $\frac{1}{3} = \frac{2}{6} = \frac{4}{12}$ and $\frac{1}{3} = \frac{3}{9}$, and so forth.

Numerically, for any fraction an equivalent fraction can be found by multiplying the numerator and denominator by the same number. For example:

$\frac{4}{7}$ is equivalent to $\frac{16}{28}$ (the numerator and denominator have been multiplied by 4)

The same applies when dividing the numerator and denominator by the same number. For example:

$\frac{36}{63}$ is equivalent to $\frac{4}{7}$ (the numerator and denominator have been divided by 9)

Finding equivalent fractions is closely linked to 'cancelling' fractions during calculations. If the numerator and denominator are 'cancelled' in order to simplify the fraction, then the new fraction will be equivalent to the original one. For example:

$\frac{6}{18}$ can be reduced to $\frac{1}{3}$ (by dividing numerator and denominator by 6)

$\frac{6}{18}$ and $\frac{1}{3}$ are equivalent fractions so would appear on a number line in the same place.

Sometimes it is easier to cancel in two or more stages:

$\frac{96}{132}$ (divide numerator and denominator by 3) $\frac{32}{44}$ (divide numerator and denominator by 4) $\frac{8}{11}$

COMPARING FRACTIONS

Comparing fractions is quite straightforward if the denominators are the same (referred to as having a **common denominator**), e.g. $\frac{5}{7}$ is bigger than $\frac{3}{7}$. This is clear as the denominator, in this case 7, indicates the number of fractional parts the unit has been divided into (sevenths here), whilst the numerator indicates the number of parts (here 5 and 3, and 5 is greater than 3). This is harder to see if the fractions have different denominators.

Is $\frac{3}{4}$ bigger than $\frac{5}{7}$? Here the denominators are 4 and 7. In order to compare them, the fractions need to be expressed in terms of units which have been divided into the same number of fractional parts, i.e. they need to have a common denominator. The lowest number which is a multiple of both 4 and 7 is 28.

$\frac{3}{4}$ is equivalent to $\frac{21}{28}$ (top and bottom multiplied by 7)

$\frac{5}{7}$ is equivalent to $\frac{20}{28}$ (top and bottom multiplied by 4)

From this it is clear that $\frac{3}{4}$ is larger than $\frac{5}{7}$.

Finding equivalent fractions, cancelling and comparing are all necessary skills when calculating using fractions.

ADDITION OF FRACTIONS

When adding fractions it is important to remember that the denominators are not added. This is quite obvious really when considering what the denominators actually represent. The denominator represents the number of parts the unit has been divided into. Taking an example adding two fractions with a common denominator gives:

$\frac{1}{4} + \frac{2}{4} = \frac{3}{4}$ this can clearly be seen from:

If the fractions to be added do not have a common denominator, then equivalent fractions need to be found which do have a common denominator to allow the addition to take place. For example:

$\frac{1}{5} + \frac{3}{4}$

The lowest common denominator is the lowest number which is a multiple of both 5 and 4, i.e. the lowest common multiple, in this case 20.

Next, work out the equivalent fractions expressed in twentieths:

$\frac{1}{5}$ – in order to achieve twentieths the denominator was multiplied by 4. To keep the fraction equivalent, the numerator must also be multiplied by 4, giving:

$\frac{1}{5} = \frac{4}{20}$

$\frac{3}{4}$ – in order to achieve twentieths the denominator was multiplied by 5. Again to ensure equivalence the numerator must be multiplied by the same, giving:

$\frac{3}{4} = \frac{15}{20}$

Rewriting the addition using equivalent fractions expressed in twentieths gives:

$\frac{4}{20} + \frac{15}{20} = \frac{19}{20}$

SUBTRACTION OF FRACTIONS

Subtracting fractions is very similar to adding them. If the denominators are the same it is very straightforward. If they do not have a common denominator, as with addition, one needs to be found in order to identify equivalent fractions to subtract. For example:

$\frac{3}{4} - \frac{1}{6}$

The lowest common denominator (or lowest common multiple) here is 12.

Expressing $\frac{3}{4}$ in twelfths gives $\frac{9}{12}$

Expressing $\frac{1}{6}$ in twelfths gives $\frac{2}{12}$

Substituting these equivalent fractions into the subtraction problem gives:

$$\frac{9}{12} - \frac{2}{12} = \frac{7}{12}$$

MULTIPLICATION OF FRACTIONS

In order to multiply fractions it is necessary to consider what is happening when you multiply any numbers. What does 2×5 actually mean? The meaning can be stated in a range of ways including 'twice 5' or 'twice as much as 5'. Consider what the meaning would be if a fractional value was substituted, e.g. $2 \times \frac{1}{4}$. This could be said to mean 'twice as much as $\frac{1}{4}$'. Therefore $\frac{1}{2} \times \frac{1}{4}$ can be read as '$\frac{1}{2}$ as much as $\frac{1}{4}$' or '$\frac{1}{2}$ of $\frac{1}{4}$'. One quarter can be shown as:

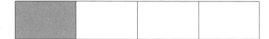

$\frac{1}{4}$ of the unit

Next, find one half of one quarter of the unit:

Here $\frac{1}{2}$ of $\frac{1}{4}$ of the unit has been revealed

This illustrates that $\frac{1}{2} \times \frac{1}{4} = \frac{1}{8}$.

Generally, it can be seen that in order to multiply the two fractions the numerators were multiplied together and the denominators were multiplied together. This can be expressed as:

$$\frac{a}{b} \times \frac{c}{d} = \frac{a \times c}{b \times d} \qquad \text{for any numbers a, b, c, d}$$

DIVISION OF FRACTIONS

In order to fully explain division of fractions, it is necessary to find a context which structures the problem clearly – one such context is food! Consider the problem $\frac{1}{2} \div 4$. This could also be written as $\frac{1}{2} \div \frac{4}{1}$.

Half a cake needs to be shared between 4 people. How much cake will each person get? Each person will get $\frac{1}{4}$ of the $\frac{1}{2}$ cake that is left, i.e $\frac{1}{8}$.

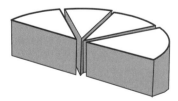

From this it can be seen that an equivalent way of writing $\frac{1}{2} \div \frac{4}{1}$ is as $\frac{1}{4}$ of $\frac{1}{2}$ or $\frac{1}{4} \times \frac{1}{2}$. Because multiplication is commutative, $\frac{1}{4} \times \frac{1}{2}$ can be rewritten as $\frac{1}{2} \times \frac{1}{4}$.

Another example: $\frac{3}{4} \div \frac{2}{3}$

This is the same as $\frac{3}{2}$ of $\frac{3}{4}$ or $\frac{3}{4} \times \frac{3}{2}$, so:

$$\frac{3}{4} \div \frac{2}{3} = \frac{3}{4} \times \frac{3}{2} = \frac{9}{8} = 1\frac{1}{8}$$

Decimals

The decimal system was popularised by John Napier (1550–1617). He was a Scottish landowner who counted mathematics as his chief hobby. He was particularly interested in trigonometry and computation. In 1614 he published the first book of logarithmic tables which had taken him 20 years to complete. He also invented Napier's bones, a calculating system using numbered rods.

Decimal fractions are an extension of place value and are not a new set of numbers. The decimal representation of a number is actually based on the fractions $\frac{1}{10}$, $\frac{1}{100}$, $\frac{1}{1000}$ etc. This should be remembered when **ordering** decimals. 0.35 and 0.09 are $\frac{35}{100}$ (35 hundredths) and $\frac{9}{100}$ (9 hundredths) respectively.

Decimal notation is used and seen with calculators, computers, money, petrol pumps and measurements, so it would seem increasingly likely that the use of fractions will become more common during conversation and certain specific occasions rather than in mathematical computation.

'I am going to cut this cake into quarters,' is easier to say than, 'I'm going to cut this cake into 0.25s!' Conversely $0.25 + 0.5 + 0.2$ is an easier calculation than $\frac{1}{4} + \frac{1}{2} + \frac{1}{5}$.

Addition and subtraction of decimal numbers is exactly the same as with whole numbers. When multiplying and dividing by powers of 10 it is important to remember that the decimal point is fixed and that 0 is used as a place holder.

	Th	H	T	U	.	$\frac{1}{10}$	$\frac{1}{100}$	$\frac{1}{1000}$
1.1 × 1000	1	1	0	0				
1.1 × 100		1	1	0				
1.1 × 10			1	1				
1.1 × 1				1	.	1		
1.1 ÷ 10				0	.	1	1	
1.1 ÷ 100				0	.	0	1	1

(Notice that the whole numbers do not require a decimal point.)

When multiplying and dividing by decimal numbers, remember that decimals are a representation of fractions so $0.1 = \frac{1}{10}$. Knowing this, work through the following calculations:

$$500 \times 0.1 = 500 \times \frac{1}{10} = 500 \div 10 = \frac{(500)}{10} = 50$$

$$500 \div 0.1 = 500 \div \frac{1}{10} = 500 \times 10 = 5000$$

It may be helpful to 'read' the calculations using multiplication of whole numbers as a 'model'.

5×2 can be interpreted as 2 groups of 5 or 5 groups of 2 (because of the commutative nature of multiplication) and the answer is 10. Similarly 500×0.1 can be seen as 500 groups of 0.1, which is 50.

$10 \div 2$ can be read as 'how many 2s in 10?' and so $500 \div 0.1$ is 'how many 0.1 s in 500?' with the answer being 5000.

It is important to have a realistic idea of the estimated answer when working with decimals. For example, the answer to 4.67×3.23 will be between 12 and 20 because $4 \times 3 = 12$ (taking the whole numbers below the decimal numbers stated) and $5 \times 4 = 20$ (taking the whole numbers above the decimal numbers stated). It is also possible to say it is approximately equal to 5×3, by rounding to the nearest whole numbers. This is particularly useful in calculations where estimation can be used to check if the answer looks to be within a sensible range.

Division solely involving whole numbers results in an answer which is smaller than the dividend. The dividend is the number that is to be divided, the divisor is the number by which the dividend is divided. For example:

dividend ⟶ $\dfrac{24}{6} = 4$ ⟵ **quotient**
divisor ⟶

When dividing two decimal numbers less than 1, the answer is a larger number. The number line can be used to illustrate examples of division and multiplication involving decimals. This is because both multiplication and division are based on the concepts of repeated addition and subtraction.

This number line illustrates $0.2 \times 4 = 0.8$ or $0.8 \div 0.2 = 4$

ADDITION AND SUBTRACTION OF DECIMALS

Because the decimal system was devised to show fractional parts within one number, through the use of the decimal point, it is very straightforward to add or subtract decimals.

Addition and subtraction are virtually the same as with whole numbers – do remember that if setting out a calculation vertically, it is vital to ensure the decimal points 'line up' to keep the place value set throughout the problem.

For example, adding 25.46 and 7.523 gives:

```
  2 5.46
+   7,523
3,2.983
```

Where attempting subtraction involving decomposition, it is important to remember that 0 is used as a place holder. For example, 25.46 − 7.523:

```
 I I4  I 5 I
2 5.460      ←——————— 0 inserted as a place holder to aid the calculation
−  7 .523
I 7 .937
```

MULTIPLICATION OF DECIMALS

Formal multiplication of decimals can be undertaken in a number of ways. Some of these methods structure the place value concept, others do not. One method, which was quite widely taught as a formal algorithm, involved completely ignoring the place value structure! This can be seen in the following working for 6.4 x 2.3:

```
     6 .4
×    2 .3
  I 9,2      ←————— Decimal point is ignored here!
  1 2 8 0
 14,.7 2     ————→  The number of digits in total after the decimal points in
                    the question is found and the decimal point is reinserted
                    to allow this number of decimal places in the answer!
```

This method obviously does nothing to develop a place value understanding for decimals. It is possible to use the standard long multiplication algorithm with decimals and structure it to keep the place value accurately determined. The same question might be attempted as follows:

```
   6.4
 ×2.3
   I .9,2    ————→   0.3 × 6.4
  1 2.8      ————→     2 × 6.4
 1 4,.7 2
```

As mentioned earlier in this chapter, it is possible to use the Gelosia method of multiplication when multiplying decimals. This method has place value built into the structure and can be infinitely extended either side of the decimal point.

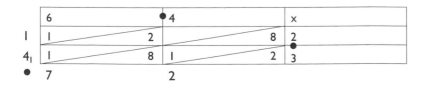

In this case to position the decimal point correctly in the answer, imagine lines extending from the decimal points in the question, one line vertical, the other horizontal. These lines meet at a diagonal. It is at the end of this diagonal that the decimal point should be placed. As can be seen in the example above, this works since extended lines from the decimal points in the questions will always meet at the diagonal separating units from tenths – place value is built into the structure.

DIVISION OF DECIMALS

Division of decimals is very straightforward providing you can divide whole numbers. If the dividend (number to be divided) is a decimal number and the divisor (number dividing into the dividend) is a whole number, the calculation is carried out in exactly the same way as for standard long division. For example, $773.112 \div 24$, using the abbreviated algorithm:

$$24 \overline{)7\,7^5 3.^5 1^3 1^7 2} \quad \begin{array}{c} 3\,2.\,2\,1\,3 \end{array}$$

In order to undertake decimal division involving a divisor that is a decimal number in the most straightforward way, it is necessary to undertake an equivalent calculation. The first thing to do is to multiply the divisor by a power of ten in order to transform it into a whole number. Having done that, the dividend must be multiplied by the same power of ten in order that the quotient will remain unchanged. For example, in order to divide 0.2 by 0.5, the divisor (in this case 0.5) needs to be changed into a whole number. To do this it must be multiplied by 10, giving 5. Having multiplied the divisor by 10 it is necessary to multiply the dividend by 10, giving 2. Why does this work? This can be shown very simply using algebra:

x divided by y is the same as $10x$ divided by $10y$ because

$$\frac{10x}{10y} = \frac{x}{y}$$

Try using this to solve $0.448 \div 0.14$:

First multiply the divisor (0.14) by 100 to make it a whole number, i.e. 14. Next multiply the dividend by the same number to ensure the quotient remains unchanged, giving $0.448 \times 100 = 44.8$. Now divide using an appropriate algorithm:

$$14 \overline{)44.^2 8} \quad \begin{array}{c} 3.\,2 \end{array}$$

CONVERTING FRACTIONS AND DECIMALS

Conversion between fractions and decimals involves some straightforward calculations. In order to convert a fraction to a decimal the fraction is simply treated as the division that it represents, e.g.:

To convert $\frac{3}{4}$ into a decimal, 3 is divided by 4, thus $\quad 4 \overline{)3.^3 0^2 0} \quad \begin{array}{c} 0.\,7\,5 \end{array}$

Converting back from a decimal to a fraction involves identifying the fractional parts represented by the decimal, e.g.:

0.75 could also be read as 7 tenths and 5 hundredths or as 75 hundredths. It is this second version, 75 hundredths where the decimal is expressed in terms of just one fractional part, that enables the fractional equivalence to be shown:

$0.75 = \frac{75}{100}$ which can be simplified by dividing top and bottom by 25 giving $\frac{3}{4}$.

Try to convert 0.125 into a fraction before looking at the workings below.

0.125 represents 125 thousandths or $\frac{125}{1000}$. This can be simplified by dividing by 125 to give $\frac{1}{8}$.

Percentages

Another way of representing fractions is as a **percentage**. The word 'percentage' comes from 'per centum' meaning 'out of a hundred'. Percentages are used to describe a proportion of a specific group. They are fractions with a denominator of 100. '58% of the class have school dinners' does not imply that the class has 100 children, but simply indicates the proportion of the children having school dinners. It allows for easy comparisons with other classes containing different numbers of children.

The equivalence of fractions, decimals and percentages can be seen if plotted on a number line.

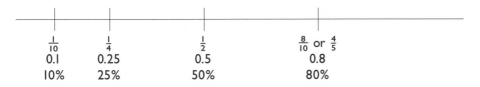

$\frac{1}{10}$	$\frac{1}{4}$	$\frac{1}{2}$	$\frac{8}{10}$ or $\frac{4}{5}$
0.1	0.25	0.5	0.8
10%	25%	50%	80%

CALCULATING PERCENTAGES
It is possible to use facts you already know to calculate some percentage problems, others may require a written method.

To find 15% of 60 it is possible to use a mental method:
    100% = 60
     10% = 6   ($\frac{1}{10}$ of 60)
      5% = 3   ($\frac{1}{2}$ of 10%)
Giving 15% of 60 = 6 + 3 = 9

Knowledge of fractions is very useful when calculating some percentages, e.g. to find 75% of 48:

    Remember 75% = $\frac{3}{4}$

    $\frac{1}{4}$ of 48 = 12
    $\frac{3}{4}$ of 48 = 36 (12 × 3)

Hence 75% of 48 = 36 (because $\frac{3}{4}$ = 75%)

Other problems require a pencil and paper calculation, e.g.:

A school has 325 pupils on roll. 64% of these pupils bring a packed lunch to school. How many children have a packed lunch?

In order to answer this, it is necessary to remember that 64% can also be represented by the fraction $\frac{64}{100}$ (**remember, percentages are fractions with a denominator of 100**).

So 64% of 325 can also be written as:

$$\frac{64}{100} \times 325$$
$$= \frac{64}{4} \times 13 \text{ (dividing 100 and 325 by 25)}$$
$$= 16 \times 13 \text{ (dividing 64 and 4 by 4)}$$
$$= 208$$

Hence 208 children bring a packed lunch to school.

Equality

Think about this

Eles is given the following numbers and expressions and asked to find as many statements about equality as possible. The numbers and expressions given are:

12, 6 + 6, 2 × 6, 24 ÷ 2

The statements she creates are:

12 = 6 + 6   6 + 6 = 12   12 = 2 × 6   2 × 6 = 12
12 = 24 ÷ 2   24 ÷ 2 = 12

What does this tell you about her understanding of equality?

One thing which is clear is that Eles does understand the symmetric property of equality. However, the transitive property is not yet understood. What subject knowledge do you need to be able to support and extend her knowledge and understanding of equality?

Equality is the mathematical idea which is expressed by the = sign. For example, if 3 is added to 4 then the answer is 7. This can be written as 3 + 4 = 7, the = sign expressing the equality of the two statements.

There are three properties of equality. They are:

- **equality is** *reflexive;*
- **equality is** *symmetric;*
- **equality is** *transitive.*

The **reflexive** property of equality simply means that a = a. For example, 4 = 4 and 627 = 627.

The **symmetric** property of equality can be expressed as 'if $x = y$ then $y = x$'. Eles was showing an understanding of this by recording both $12 = 6 + 6$ and $6 + 6 = 12$.

The **transitive** property means that if $x = y$ and $y = z$ then $x = z$. Using the statements given to Eles, this can be shown as follows:

If $6 + 6 = 12$ and $12 = 24 \div 2$ then $6 + 6 = 24 \div 2$

Inequalities

An **inequality** simply states that one number is greater or smaller than another. For example, '6 is less than 10' is an inequality and can be written as $6 < 10$. The symbol $<$ means 'less than' when reading left to right. It is also possible to say '10 is greater than 6' which can be written as $10 > 6$. This time the symbol $>$ means 'greater than' when reading left to right. From this it can be seen that $6 < 10$ means the same as $10 > 6$.

Other symbols which may be encountered when dealing with inequalities are $\leqslant$ which means 'less than or equal to', $\geqslant$ which means 'greater than or equal to' and $\neq$ which means 'not equal to'. You have already encountered use of the 'not equal to' symbol '$\neq$' when considering the laws of arithmetic.

For more information on this symbol, see page 9 for the section on laws of arithmetic.

Inequalities can be manipulated in a similar way to equations. If a number is added or subtracted from both sides of the inequality, then the inequality is preserved, i.e. the statement is still true, e.g.:

$$6 < 10$$
$$6 + 5 < 10 + 5 \quad \text{(5 is added to each side of the inequality)}$$
$$11 < 15 \quad \text{(the inequality is preserved, the statement is still true)}$$

Multiplication and division need to be treated slightly differently, depending on whether the number which the inequality is multiplied by, or divided by, is positive or negative.

If an inequality is multiplied or divided by a positive number then the inequality is preserved, e.g.:

$$6 < 10$$
$$6 \times 2 < 10 \times 2 \quad \text{(both sides of the inequality are multiplied by 2)}$$
$$12 < 20 \quad \text{(the inequality is preserved)}$$

And division gives:

$$6 < 10$$
$$6 \div 2 < 10 \div 2 \qquad \text{(both sides of the inequality are divided by 2)}$$
$$3 < 5 \qquad \text{(the inequality is preserved)}$$

However, if the inequality is multiplied or divided by a negative number then the inequality is reversed, e.g.:

$$6 < 10$$
$$6 \times -2 < 10 \times -2$$
$$-12 < -20$$

This is not true – the inequality has been reversed, hence:

$$-12 > -20$$

Knowing this, it is possible to reverse the inequality symbol at the appropriate place within the calculation, e.g.:

$$6 < 10$$
$$6 \div -2 > 10 \div -2$$
$$-3 > -5$$

Inequalities are frequently encountered within the context of algebra, e.g. $x < 6$ means that x can take any value less than 6. However, if it is written as $x \leqslant 6$ this means x can take any value less than *or equal to* 6. These can be represented on a number line as:

This number line represents $x < 6$. The empty circle at 6 indicates that the value of x cannot be equal to 6.

This number line represents $x \leqslant 6$. The solid circle at 6 indicates that the value of x can be equal to 6.

Algebraic inequalities can be solved in exactly the same way as algebraic equations more generally. For example, consider $x + 4 > 6$:

$$x + 4 > 6$$
$$x > 6 - 4 \qquad \text{(4 is subtracted from both sides)}$$
$$x > 2$$

Hence x is greater than 2.

Recurring decimals

Max was asked to calculate a value for $\frac{1}{3}$. The answer given was 0.3.

What does this tell you about his understanding of recurring decimals?

It is clear that Max does not yet understand the conventions for expressing recurring decimals. What subject knowledge do you need to be able to teach him effectively?

Quite frequently in calculations decimal answers arise that go on forever. These are called **recurring decimals**. Examples include:

$\frac{1}{3} = 0.33333\ldots$

$\frac{10}{11} = 0.90909090\ldots$

In order to record that the decimal recurs without having to write them as above, dots are used to indicate the cycle of digits that is recurring. So the above would more formally be recorded as:

$\frac{1}{3} = 0.\dot{3}$ $\qquad\qquad\qquad$ $\frac{10}{11} = 0.\dot{9}\dot{0}$

This indicates that in the first example the 3 recurs, while in the second example the 90 recurs.

Some recurring decimals have longer cycles of digits recurring, e.g.:

$\frac{2}{7} = 0.2857142857142\ldots$

To write this using conventional notation gives:

$\frac{2}{7} = 0.\dot{2}8571\dot{4}$ indicating that the cycle of digits 285714 recurs.

Recurring decimals form part of a group of numbers known as the **rational numbers**.

Rational and irrational numbers

Recurring decimals form part of the set of rational numbers because they can be written as a fraction. The set of rational numbers includes all numbers that can be written as fractions. This includes all integers, all finite decimals, all recurring decimals, the square roots of perfect squares, e.g. $\sqrt{16}$ and $\sqrt{(\frac{9}{25})}$ and all other vulgar fractions.

Irrational numbers are those numbers that cannot be expressed in fractional form. Such numbers are π and other numbers involving π, for example 6π; roots that cannot be calculated exactly, e.g. $\sqrt{2}$, $\sqrt{5}$, $\sqrt[3]{7}$, and other numbers involving these roots, e.g. $6 \times \sqrt{2}$. In fact, all square roots other than those of perfect squares are irrational, as are most cube roots.

The set of rational numbers and the set of irrational numbers together make up the **real number** system. Every real number is represented by a point on the number line and conversely, every point on the number line represents a real (i.e. rational or irrational) number. So the number line has no gaps along it.

Index form

Think about this

Andrew was asked to find an answer for 5^2. The answer that was given was 10.

What does this tell you about his understanding of index form?

It is clear that Andrew does not understand what the index, in this case 2, actually means. What subject knowledge do you need, to be able to extend his understanding of index notation?

Square numbers are the product of two equal factors, e.g. 2×2, 3×3, 4×4.

Cube numbers are the product of three equal factors, e.g. $1 \times 1 \times 1$, $2 \times 2 \times 2$, $3 \times 3 \times 3$.

But what is index form or index notation?

Index form is a concise way of writing multiplication of a number by itself, so $10 \times 10 \times 10 \times 10$ can be written as 10^4.

4 is the **index**

10 is the **base** $\longrightarrow$ $10^4 = 10,000$ $\longleftarrow$ 10,000 is the 4th **power** of 10 (product of repeated multiplication)

Index form is also frequently encountered within algebraic expressions, e.g. $a^3 \times a^2$. It is interesting to consider what happens to the indices (plural of index) within this multiplication. First it is necessary to consider what the expression actually represents.

$$a^3 \times a^2 = (a \times a \times a) \times (a \times a)$$
$$= a \times a \times a \times a \times a$$
$$= a^5$$

In effect the indices have been added.

Consider division:

$$a^6 \div a^3 = \frac{a \times a \times a \times \cancel{a} \times \cancel{a} \times \cancel{a}}{\cancel{a} \times \cancel{a} \times \cancel{a}}$$
$$= a \times a \times a$$
$$= a^3$$

So for division, in effect the indices have been subtracted.

An interesting fact concerning **index notation** – consider the pattern of 'powers of 2'. It could start at $2^1 = 2$, $2^2 = 4$, $2^3 = 8$, $2^4 = 16$, ... But what about 2^0? Any number raised to the power 0 gives the answer 1. Consider why this is the case.

Start with a^3. To move down the sequence to the preceding term it is necessary to divide by a, giving a^2. To move down the sequence again divide by a again, giving a^1. To move down the sequence again to a^0, it is necessary to divide a^1 by a. We already know that $a^1 = a$, so $a^1 \div a = a \div a = 1$. This can be extended into negative powers, a^{-1} being $a^0 \div a = 1 \div a = \frac{1}{a}$.

Standard form

Standard form is sometimes called **standard index form** as it uses powers of 10, i.e. 10 expressed in index form (see above).

Standard form is a shorthand way of writing very small and very large numbers that would require a huge number of digits if written in full. It can be used to express large numbers such as the vast distances of planets from Earth, or small numbers such as the minute scientific measurements within an atom.

In order to express a number in standard form it is written as a number between 1 and 10 then multiplied by a power of 10. The power of 10 is called the **order of magnitude** and indicates the overall size of the number. The number between 1 and 10 gives greater detail about the overall number. For example:

6000000 written in standard form is 6×10^6
0.0000000759 written in standard form is 7.59×10^{-8}

As can be seen from the above, multiplying by a positive power of 10 gives a number greater than 1, whilst multiplying be a negative power of 10 gives a number less than 1.

It is interesting to note a certain 'symmetry' in the index notation for the powers of 10 used in standard form:

1 is 10^0	$\frac{1}{1}$	is 10^0
10 is 10^1	$\frac{1}{10}$	is 10^{-1}
100 is 10^2	$\frac{1}{100}$	is 10^{-2}
1000 is 10^3	$\frac{1}{1000}$	is 10^{-3}

Ratio and proportion

Think about this

Neve is asked to identify the proportion of white tiles in the following tiling pattern:

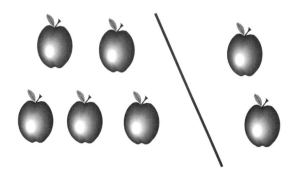

She says 1 in 3 of the tiles is white.

What does this tell you about her understanding of proportion?

It is clear that Neve might be confusing ratio and proportion. What subject knowledge do you need to effectively support and extend this child's knowledge and understanding of ratio and proportion?

Ratio is the comparative size of quantities, numbers or measures of the same kind. It is written either as a:b or as a fraction $\frac{a}{b}$, e.g. 3:5 or $\frac{3}{5}$.

If one bottle holds 200 ml and another holds 400 ml then the second one is twice as big or they have a ratio of 200:400 or 1:2.

As can be seen in the above example, the ratio of one number to another remains the same if both numbers are multiplied or divided by the same number. This is an **equivalent** ratio.

But this is not the case if numbers are added or subtracted to both numbers, e.g.:

$$1:2 \neq 2:3 \quad \text{and} \quad 5:4 \neq 4:3$$

Partitioning underlies ratio. For example, if two children shared 7 apples so that child A received 5 apples and child B received 2 apples, their sharing is in a ratio of 5:2.

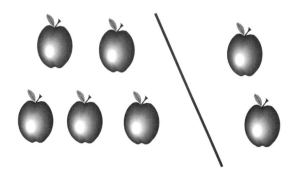

Child A would receive $\frac{5}{2}$ times more than child B. With more apples to share, child A would always receive 2.5 times as many apples as child B. This demonstrates the multiplicative structure of ratio:

child A	child B
5	2
10	4
15	6
20	8

Ratio can be used to solve other problems, for example:

If 5 cakes cost 35p, how much will 3 cakes cost?

Using the ratio 5:3 gives $\frac{5}{3} = \frac{35}{a}$. The value for a can be found by simply rearranging the equation:

$$\frac{5}{3} = \frac{35}{a}$$

$$a = 35 \times \frac{3}{5}$$

$$a = 21$$

So the cost of 3 cakes is 21p.

A **scale factor** can be expressed as a ratio. Imagine Tom has £10 and Joe has £30. In order to have the same amount as Joe, Tom would have to multiply his money by 3, £10 × 3 = £30. The amount has been increased by a scale factor, in this case 1 × 3 or 1:3.

Similarly the ratio structure can be used to **compare** two quantities. An example of this would be the two children, Tom with 20p and Joe with 60p. Joe has 3 times as much money as Tom because 60 ÷ 20 is 3. (Tom's 20p would have to be increased by three to equal Joe's 60p.)

Proportion is sometimes mistakenly used to mean ratio but proportion compares part of a quantity with the whole. So a ratio of 1:3 results in proportions of 1 out of 4 and 3 out of 4. This is the mistake Neve was making.

Imagine a recipe for raisin cup cakes requires 110g of flour, 60g of sugar, 100g of butter, 80g of raisins and 2 eggs. This recipe will make 12 cakes. How much of each ingredient would be required if 18 cakes were needed? In order to keep the proportions the same, and therefore keep the cakes edible, the ingredients need to be increased in the ratio 18:12 or 3:2. 110g of flour represents 2 within the ratio 3:2, so to calculate the new value it is necessary to divide by 2, then multiply by 3 giving 165g. Doing the same for the other ingredients gives: 90g of sugar, 150g butter, 120g raisins and 3 eggs.

It is possible to express ratios as percentages (as well as fractions and decimals):

$$2:5 = \frac{2}{5} = 0.4 = \frac{40}{100} = 40\%$$

Number:

a summary of key points

_____ *Prior to attempting to solve any complex expressions, it is necessary to know the order of precedence of the operations. This order can be summarised as BODMAS.*

_____ *There are certain structural laws underpinning arithmetic. Addition and multiplication are both commutative and associative. Multiplication is distributive over addition and subtraction. Division is right distributive over addition and subtraction.*

_____ *Our decimal place value system uses only ten digits. The position of a digit relative to any other digits in the number determines its value. The larger groupings are always on the left. Numbers are read from left to right.*

_____ *The four number operations are related to each other in specific ways. Addition is the inverse of subtraction and vice versa. Multiplication and division are the inverse of each other. Multiplication can be seen as repeated addition and division as repeated subtraction.*

_____ *The use of fractions falls into two main areas, as a measurement and as an operator on another number.*

_____ *Decimals form an extension to our place value system.*

_____ *Percentages can be considered as another way of representing fractions. They are fractions with a denominator of 100. Percentages can also be represented as decimals.*

_____ *The set of rational numbers and the set of irrational numbers together make up the real numbers.*

_____ *Standard form allows very large and very small numbers to be written concisely.*

_____ *Ratio and proportion make use of a multiplicative structure to solve problems.*

✓ Self-assessment questions

1 Use the order of precedence of the operations (BODMAS) to calculate the following:

$10 \div 2 + 8 \times 3 - \frac{1}{2} \text{ of } 6 + (4 - 2)$

2 Reduce these fractions to their simplest forms:

(a) $\frac{7}{14}$ (b) $\frac{40}{46}$ (c) $\frac{121}{187}$ (d) $\frac{21}{7}$

3 What are the answers to:

(a) $\frac{1}{2} + \frac{5}{7}$ (b) $\frac{3}{5} + \frac{2}{6}$

(c) $\frac{9}{11} - \frac{1}{3}$ (d) $\frac{3}{4} - \frac{1}{12}$

(e) $\frac{1}{5} \times \frac{3}{4}$ (f) $\frac{3}{10} \times \frac{1}{9}$

(g) $\frac{1}{9} \div \frac{2}{3}$ (h) $\frac{4}{7} \div \frac{21}{24}$

4 Convert the following to percentages:

(a) $\frac{3}{5}$ (b) $\frac{7}{10}$ (c) $\frac{1}{8}$

5 Calculate the following:

(a) $17\frac{1}{2}\%$ of 68   (b) 75% of 88   (c) 60% of 70

6 Solve the following inequalities:

(a) $3x \geqslant 15$ (b) $-3x \geqslant 9$ (c) $4x + 3 < 18$

7 Write down the following in standard form:

(a) 400   (b) 619 000   (c) 8412.3
(d) 0.015   (e) 0.000000789

Further reading

Askew, M. (1999) *Teaching Primary Mathematics: a Guide for Newly Qualified and Student Teachers*. London: Hodder and Stoughton.

Haylock, D. (2001) *Mathematics Explained for Primary Teachers*. London: Paul Chapman Publishing. As the title suggests, this book explains much of the content of the primary mathematics curriculum. It also addresses key teaching points and gives opportunities to try some self-assessment questions in each area, to further support your subject knowledge development.

Merttens, R. (ed.) (1996) *Teaching Numeracy: Maths in the Primary Classroom*. Leamington Spa: Scholastic. This book looks at developing numeracy starting from the early years. It also covers areas of current debate including numeracy and calculators as well as considering bilingual children learning number.

Nunes, T. and Bryant, P. (1996) *Children Doing Mathematics*. Oxford: Blackwell. This book focuses on children learning mathematics and the conditions that promote this learning. It draws on recent research in children's mathematical understanding to highlight ways of advancing their learning.

Thompson, I. (ed.) (1997) *Teaching and Learning Early Number*. Buckingham: Open University Press. This book considers many of the issues and debates surrounding young children's learning of number. It addresses issues from both a theoretical and practical point of view.

Thompson, I. (ed.) (1999) *Issues in Teaching Numeracy in Primary Schools*. Buckingham: Open University Press. This book addresses many issues of current debate within the development of numeracy in schools. It tackles the direct classroom based issues as well as considering children as learners and how to develop appropriate visual images to support the development of numeracy.

Williams, E. and Shuard, H. (1997) *Primary Mathematics Today*. Harlow: Longman. This book is an extremely comprehensive text covering all aspects of primary mathematics. It supports subject knowledge development very effectively while at the same time considering pedagogical issues and clearly detailing progression.

Introduction

Algebra is a word that is frequently misunderstood or even feared. So, what is algebra? It is certainly about the manipulation of symbols, but that is only a small part, at the very end of the mathematical thinking. Before the symbols come the patterns – seeing, interpreting and expressing patterns is at the heart of algebra. How the patterns are expressed eventually leads to the symbolic form, having passed through diagrams or pictures and words. Representing these patterns symbolically leads to the study of equations and functions, and representing these equations and functions leads to graphing. An understanding of equations, functions and graphs is very important as it allows us to represent some aspects of mathematics in a clear and concise way. By using unknowns to write an equation, or within a function, it is possible to see the range of answers easily from one statement. Equally, representing the **data** as a graph allows trends to be identified and information to be interpreted from a visual image, which is often a lot more straightforward than looking solely at the numbers.

Professional Standards for QTS

 ### 2.1b

To achieve QTS you need to have a secure knowledge and understanding of the mathematics content of the National Curriculum for Key Stages 1 and 2 and the methods and expectations set out in the National Numeracy Strategy. For algebra, equations, functions and graphs this includes:

- *Number operations and algebra;*
  - *finding factors and multiples of simple algebraic expressions;*
  - *constructing general statements;*
  - *manipulating simple algebraic expressions and using formulae;*
  - *knowing when numerical expressions and algebraic expressions are equivalent;*
  - *number sequences, their n^{th} terms and their sums.*
- *Equations, functions and graphs:*
  - *forming equations and solving linear and simultaneous linear equations, finding exact solutions;*
  - *interpreting functions and finding inverses of simple functions;*
  - *representing functions graphically and algebraically;*
  - *understanding the significance of gradients and intercepts;*
  - *interpreting graphs, and using them to solve equations.*

You may find it helpful to read through the appropriate section of the Handbook that accompanies the Standards for the award of QTS for clarification and support.

Curriculum Guidance for the Foundation Stage, the National Curriculum and the National Numeracy Strategy

The Curriculum Guidance for the Foundation Stage recognises the importance of certain key skills in mathematical development. The areas identified include seeking patterns and working with numbers. This encourages an early introduction to algebra generally as well as leading into the specific areas of equations, functions and graphs.

Within the Mathematics National Curriculum the Programmes of Study clearly state the knowledge, skills and understanding which are to be taught throughout the Key Stages. These are closely linked to the Key Objectives identified for each year group within the NNS *Framework for Teaching Mathematics*.

At Key Stage I, children 'create and describe number patterns'. They also start to recognise sequences and are introduced to solving numerical equations containing unknowns, in both written and mental forms. They are expected to understand and investigate general statements. They start to solve problems by using 'charts to sort, classify and organise information' (Maths NC, 1999).

During Key Stage 2, children further develop their understanding of these concepts. They are expected to understand and investigate general statements and search for patterns in their results. They are expected to recognise and describe number patterns and make predictions and general statements. They start to describe functional relationships and 'recognise, represent and interpret simple number relationships' (Maths NC, 1999) by constructing formulae in words and then in symbols. They use graphs to extend their understanding of the number system, including integers, fractions and decimals, and to explore simple algebraic ideas. These aspects of mathematics are reflected in the NNS Key Objectives, particularly in the emphasis on patterns, number sequences, solving numerical problems, and interpreting graphs to solve problems.

RESEARCH SUMMARY

Falkner, Levi and Carpenter (1999) researched children's understanding of the 'equals' sign. Understanding equality is important if children are going to be able to manipulate algebraic equations effectively. They found that children interpreted 'equals' as meaning 'carry out the calculation preceding the sign', regardless of what comes after it. For example, when asking sixth grade children: $8 + 4 = ? + 5$, all 145 children got the answer wrong. 84% said 12, 14% said 17 and 2% had other answers, none correct. The implications of this lack of understanding of equality are great for developing algebraic understanding in the future. They concluded that it is necessary to ensure children understand that equality is a relationship rather than a signal to do something.

For more information on understanding equality, see page 30 for the section on equality.

Knowledge and understanding

The area of mathematics known as algebra derives its name from a book entitled *Hisab al-jabr wa'l muqabalah* by Muhammad al-Khwarizmi (c.780 – c.850). The title translates as 'Calculation by Restoration and Reduction'. **Restoration** means simplifying an equation by performing the same operation on each side and **reduction** involves combining different parts of the equation to make it simpler. Muhammad al-Khwarizmi's ideas have been so influential in the world of mathematics that the word *al-jabr* in the title of his book has become the *algebra* of today.

Although Muhammad al-Khwarizmi has been extremely influential in the area of algebra, the ideas have been known about since ancient Egyptian times. The Rhind Papyrus is named after the Scottish Egyptologist Alexander Henry Rhind who acquired it in 1858. It is also sometimes called the Ahmes Papyrus after the scribe who wrote it in about 1650 BCE. He stated that it was copied from an even earlier document of around 2000 BCE. It is now kept in the British Museum. This papyrus contains the first documentary evidence of the use of algebra. Unknowns are represented as symbols within simple problems for solving. Compared to algebra today it is very basic, but it is important to remember that the knowledge and understanding of today has been built up over a considerable amount of time from foundations like the Rhind Papyrus.

Algebraic expressions

Think about this

As the result of an investigation two children, Zoe and David, establish the following relationship, 'multiply a number by itself, add two then halve'. They decide to represent the relationship algebraically. They come up with the following solutions:

Zoe: $\dfrac{n \times n + 2}{2}$

David: $\frac{1}{2}(n^2 + 2)$

Zoe argues that their answers are different yet they both insist they are correct. What does this tell you about their understanding of algebraic expressions?

It is clear that David has a more sophisticated understanding of representing and manipulating algebraic expressions. Zoe has expressed the general relationship algebraically but, as yet, is unable to manipulate the expression in order to simplify it. What knowledge do you need to be able to effectively support and extend these children as they develop their understanding of forming and manipulating algebraic expressions?

SIMPLIFYING ALGEBRAIC EXPRESSIONS
In order to simplify algebraic expressions it is necessary to gather together or combine **terms** and powers wherever possible.

Terms are algebraic quantities that are separated from each other in expressions by + or − signs, e.g.:

$$2n^2 + 4n - 6$$

Terms

Like terms are multiples of the same algebraic quantity. Hence if terms are not of the same algebraic quantity they are **unlike** terms. For example:

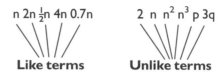

Like terms   **Unlike terms**

Hence in order to simplify $(4n)^2 + 3n - 2 + 4n^2 - n + 7$ it is necessary first to identify like terms, then to combine them. It is often easier to group the like terms together within the expression then combine them.

$(4n)^2 + 3n - 2 + 4n^2 - n + 7$
$(4n \times 4n) + 3n - 2 + 4n^2 - n + 7$
$16n^2 + 3n - 2 + 4n^2 - n + 7$
$16n^2 + 4n^2 + 3n - n - 2 + 7$
$20n^2 + 2n + 5$

Another useful strategy when simplifying expressions is to find **factors**. When considering numbers, any whole number that divides a given number exactly is called a **factor** of that number. This can be extended into the consideration of algebraic terms.

To find the factors of 4ab it is necessary to find all the terms which divide 4ab exactly, i.e.:

1, 2, 4, a, b, 2a, 2b, 4a, 4b, ab, 2ab, 4ab

Now consider how the following might be simplified:

$8a^2 - ab + 4a^2 + 5ab$

First group like terms within the expression:

$8a^2 + 4a^2 - ab + 5ab$

Next combine like terms:

$12a^2 + 4ab$

Next identify a factor common to both the terms. The factor chosen is normally the highest common factor. 4a will divide exactly into $12a^2$ and 4ab (it is also the highest common factor of the terms) giving:

$4a(3a + b)$

Generally, to simplify expressions, combine terms and find factors.

General statements

Think about this

Josh is asked to describe the sets of numbers that would be generated by the general statements 2n and 2n + 1.

The following answers were given:

> *2n represents the set of square numbers.*
> *2n + 1 represents the set of square numbers plus one.*

What does this tell you about Josh's ability to interpret these general statements?

It is clear that Josh has misinterpreted the meaning of 2n in both cases. The answers clearly indicate a belief that it represents n × n or n^2. What knowledge do you need to be able to effectively support and develop his understanding of general statements?

USING ALGEBRA TO DESCRIBE SEQUENCES

It is possible to describe sequences briefly using algebra. The following sequence:

3, 6, 9, 12, 15, ...

can be expressed as a general statement for multiples of three. To do this it is necessary to give each term a position in the sequence and find a relationship between the position and the term. In this case:

position: 1   2   3   4   5   ...   n
term: 3   6   9   12   15   ...   ?

To find the nth term it is necessary to look at the previous terms. It can clearly be seen that each term is equal to 3 multiplied by the position of the term. So the nth term here is 3 multiplied by n or 3n.

There are some rules which can be applied consistently when trying to establish general terms. Firstly look at the difference between the terms. This can give a big clue to help identify the general term, e.g.:

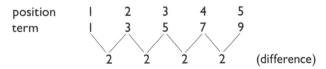

position   1   2   3   4   5
term   1   3   5   7   9
              2   2   2   2   (difference)

The fact that the difference is always 2 means that the general term will involve multiplication by 2. The only thing left to decide is, having multiplied the position by 2, what else needs to take place in order to arrive at the correct value for the term. In the above case it can be seen that, having multiplied by 2, 1 is then subtracted, giving 2n − 1.

Does this hold true for sequences with other differences?

Yes it does. Look at the following sequences. Try to work out their general terms.

position	1	2	3	4	5
term	1	4	7	10	13

position	1	2	3	4	5
term	5	9	13	17	21

Taking the first example, it can be seen that the difference between the terms is always 3. This indicates that the general case will involve multiplication by 3. What else is being done to the position number to achieve the term? Here 2 is being subtracted. This means the general term is 3n − 2.

In the second example, the difference is always 4, indicating that the position number will be multiplied by 4. Having multiplied by 4, 1 is then added, giving a general statement of 4n + 1.

This leads to a general case for all linear sequences which have a common difference (d):

$$a_n = dn + c$$

where a_n is the general term, d is the common difference and c is a constant.

But differences are not always the same. What can be established about a sequence if the difference between the terms is not the same?

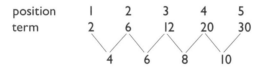

By looking at this it can be seen that the difference in each case is not the same. However, the difference in the differences is the same!

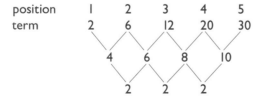

This fact indicates that the general statement is quadratic, i.e. it will contain a value for n multiplied by itself, i.e. n^2. Applying this to the above example, it is clear that the position is squared and then the position number is added to that answer, giving a general term $n^2 + n$. This can be neatly expressed as $n(n + 1)$.

This argument can be extended for greater powers of n.

SEQUENCES – EXTENSION

The above explanation can be extended to offer a fuller description of this method. The method uses equivalent numerical and algebraic expressions.

Consider the following sequence:

position (n)	1	2	3	4	5
term	6	17	34	57	86

         11   17   23   29   (first difference)

           6   6   6   (second difference)

The fact that the sequence has a common second difference indicates that it is a quadratic, i.e. contains n^2. The general form of a quadratic expression is:

$$an^2 + bn + c \text{ (where a, b and c are constants)}$$

Substituting n = 1, 2, 3, 4, 5 into the general expression gives:

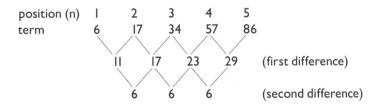

position (n)	1	2	3	4	5
term	$a + b + c$	$4a + 2b + c$	$9a + 3b + c$	$16a + 4b + c$	$25a + 5b + c$

    $3a + b$ $5a + b$ $7a + b$ $9a + b$ (first difference)

       $2a$ $2a$ $2a$ (second difference)

These two sequences and their differences are equivalent, one is the general case of the other.

By looking at the second differences it can be seen that $2a = 6$, so $a = 3$.

Substitution can now be used to calculate values for b and c. Looking at the first differences and taking the difference between the n = 1 and n = 2 terms, it can be seen that $3a + b = 11$. Substituting $a = 3$ gives $b = 2$.

Finally, looking at the first terms, it can be seen that $a + b + c = 6$. Substituting $a = 3$ and $b = 2$ gives $c = 1$.

Hence the general or n^{th} term is:

$$3n^2 + 2n + 1$$

This can be extended for other powers of n, e.g. a cubic expression has the general form $an^3 + bn^2 + cn + d$. This substitution method can be used here equally effectively.

For more information on conjecture, see page 121 for the section on levels of proof.

USING ALGEBRA TO PROVE GENERAL STATEMENTS

In mathematics it is possible to use summing to prove general statements and also **conjectures**. A conjecture is a hypothesis, something that has been surmised or deduced.

One such instance is stating that adding consecutive odd numbers, starting at 1, will result in the square numbers, i.e.:

$$
\begin{array}{ccccc}
1 & = & 1 & = & 1^2 \\
1 + 3 & = & 4 & = & 2^2 \\
1 + 3 + 5 & = & 9 & = & 3^2 \\
1 + 3 + 5 + 7 & = & 16 & = & 4^2
\end{array}
$$

In order to prove this, it is necessary first to construct the general sequence of odd numbers (use the difference method above if necessary):

position	1	2	3	...	$(n-2)$	$(n-1)$	n
term	1	3	5	...	$(2n-5)$	$(2n-3)$	$(2n-1)$

If the sum of the first n odd numbers is S, then:

$$S = 1 + 3 + 5 + ... + (2n - 5) + (2n - 3) + (2n - 1)$$

The order of the expression that is equal to S can be written in reverse order without changing the value due to the commutative nature of addition:

$$S = (2n - 1) + (2n - 3) + (2n - 5) + ... + 5 + 3 + 1$$

If these two values for S are added together a value for 2S is achieved:

$$2S = (1+(2n-1))+(3+(2n-3))+(5+(2n-5))+...+((2n-5)+5)+((2n-3)+3)+((2n-1)+1)$$
$$2S = 2n + 2n + 2n + ... + 2n + 2n + 2n$$
$$2S = n \times 2n$$
$$2S = 2n^2$$
$$S = n^2$$

This shows that the sum of consecutive odd numbers, starting at 1, will result in a square number being generated.

Linear and simultaneous linear equations

Think about this

Lisa, in Year 6, is asked the following extension question:

If I go into a shop and buy two footballs and one tennis ball the cost is £3.00. If I buy one football and three tennis balls the cost is £2.75. How much do the football and tennis ball cost individually?

She decides the following: football £1
                                 tennis ball £1

What does this tell you about her understanding of this problem?

It is clear that Lisa has not understood that both equations are required in order to solve this problem. She has merely selected numbers that would fit the first equation without using the second equation to inform her answer. What subject knowledge would you require to be able to extend Lisa's understanding?

An **equation** is a statement that two **expressions** are equal, e.g. $y = x + 2$. An **expression** is a general term used to describe mathematical terms, e.g. x^2. A **linear equation** takes the form:

$$ay + bx + c = 0$$

In the example $y = x + 2$, what are the values for a, b and c?

To work this out, it is necessary to rearrange the equation:

$$y = x + 2$$
$$y - x - 2 = 0$$

From this it is clear that $a = 1$, $b = -1$ and $c = -2$.

Because a linear equation does not involve any powers greater than 1, it can always be represented as a straight line graph. Equations involving greater powers of x are curves.

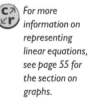

For more information on representing linear equations, see page 55 for the section on graphs.

SIMULTANEOUS LINEAR EQUATIONS

Lisa was attempting to solve **simultaneous linear equations**. Simultaneous linear equations are two linear equations which have a common solution. This means that for both equations, one value for x and the corresponding value for y, is common to them both. If the two equations were drawn on a graph, the lines would cross at the point where the values for the two equations were the same.

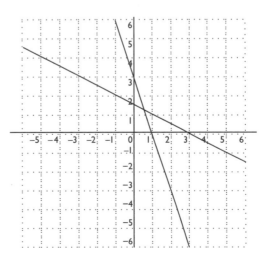

But how else can this problem be solved?

There are various ways of solving simultaneous linear equations. The first point to remember, and the point forgotten by Lisa, is that both equations are needed to find the solution.

Lisa attempted to 'guess' the answer. This is a valid method but requires the two equations in order to check the accuracy of the 'guess'. Once a 'guess' has been made, the next attempt can be refined in light of the outcome, gradually getting nearer and nearer until the answer is found. This method of trying an answer and learning something which is then applied to the next attempt can be described as '**trial and improvement**'. This is a much more positive expression than 'trial and error', which implies a mistake. Our phrase implies that learning is taking place in light of previous attempts. How might Lisa use trial and improvement to solve the problem?

> two footballs and one tennis ball cost £3.00
> one football and three tennis balls cost £2.75

Let the cost of the football be a pounds and the cost of the tennis ball b pounds.

The above equations can now be rewritten as

$$2a + b = 3.00$$
$$a + 3b = 2.75$$

Lisa's pattern of guesses might look something like this:

a	b	$2a + b$	$a + 3b$
1.00	1.00	3.00	4.00
1.15	0.70	3.00	3.25
1.25	0.50	3.00	2.75

So the prices are £1.25 for a football and 50p for a tennis ball.

There are other ways that you might choose to solve simultaneous equations yourself. One of these involves eliminating one of the unknowns. To do this it is necessary to multiply one of the equations to ensure there is an equal number of a particular unknown in both equations.

Let these two equations be called equation (1) and equation (2), i.e.

$$2a + b = 3.00 \quad (1)$$
$$a + 3b = 2.75 \quad (2)$$

If equation (1) is multiplied by 3 then both equations will have $3b$:

$$6a + 3b = 9.00 \quad (1) \times 3$$

If equation (2) is now subtracted from this new equation, the unknown $3b$ will be eliminated:

$$\begin{array}{rcl} 6a + 3b & = & 9.00 \\ a + 3b & = & 2.75 \\ \hline 5a & = & 6.25 \\ a & = & 1.25 \end{array}$$

If the value for a is substituted back into equation (1) it will be possible to calculate the value for b:

$$\begin{array}{rcll} 2a + b & = & 3.00 & (1) \\ 2.50 + b & = & 3.00 & \\ b & = & 0.50 & \end{array}$$

Hence the football costs £1.25 and the tennis ball costs 50p.

Substituting a value in an equation, as in the final step above, can be used at the outset. This next method uses one of the equations to express one unknown in terms of the other unknown. This new expression is then substituted in the other equation, which is rearranged to find a solution, e.g.:

$$\begin{array}{rcll} 2a + b & = & 3.00 & (1) \\ a + 3b & = & 2.75 & (2) \end{array}$$

Rearranging equation (2) gives:

$$a = 2.75 - 3b$$

This value for a is now substituted back into equation (1):

$$\begin{array}{rcl} 2(2.75 - 3b) + b & = & 3.00 \\ 5.50 - 6b + b & = & 3.00 \\ 5b & = & 2.50 \\ b & = & 0.50 \end{array}$$

Substituting this value for b back into equation (2) gives:

$$\begin{array}{rcl} a + 3b & = & 2.75 \\ a + 1.50 & = & 2.75 \\ a & = & 1.25 \end{array}$$

So the football costs £1.25 and the tennis ball costs 50p.

Functions and mappings

Luke is asked to identify the function in this problem:

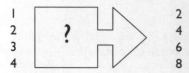

He decides that consecutive numbers are being added.

What does this tell you about his understanding of expressing functions?

First, it can be seen that Luke has expressed in words the effect of multiplying consecutive numbers by two. However, he failed to express this as a functional relationship. What knowledge do you need to be able to effectively support and extend Luke's understanding of functions?

A **function** is a rule which changes or **maps** one number on to another. Functions or **mappings** can be represented in a range of different ways. The example above shows one representation. This idea of a 'function machine' is often found in primary schools. The number 1 is the input. It is put into the machine which then acts upon it with a consistent rule, in this case x2, to give 2 as the output. 2 is input to have 4 as the output, 3 to output 6, and so on.

These relations can also be shown as two sets, e.g.:

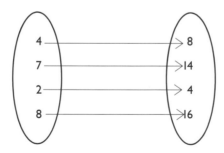

The first set (input) is also known as the **domain**. The second set (output) is known as the **range**.

Many functional relationships have a one-to-one relation, i.e. each member of the domain corresponds to one member of the range. Other functional relationships have a many-to-one relation, e.g.:

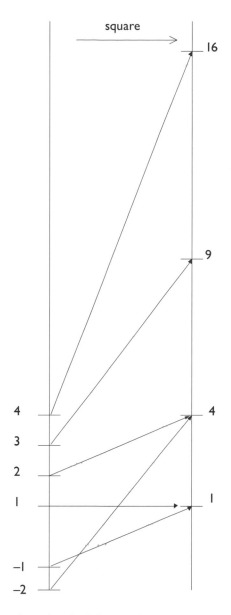

It is important to remember that, whether one-to-one or many-to-one, each member of the domain only ever corresponds to one member of the range.

Almost all the graphs children draw in school will be graphs of linear functions, i.e. for each value of the x-axis there is only one value on the y-axis.

For more information on graphs, see page 55.

Functions can also be used to represent the relationships when shapes are trans-formed. When a shape is transformed, e.g. translated, rotated, reflected or enlarged, each point on the shape is mapped onto another point.

Functions can be written in a number of ways. They are often represented with the letters f and g. Taking the example (left) of 'squaring', this could be written:

$$f \text{ changes } x \text{ into } x^2$$

or

$$y = x^2$$

or

$$f : x \longrightarrow x^2$$

or

$$f(x) = x^2$$

Both x and y are variables, but x is said to be the **independent variable** and y is the **dependent variable** because x can take any number, but the value of y depends upon the value of x.

Consider the following function:

$$f(x) = 2x + 1$$

What would be the values for f(x) corresponding to:

$$x = 1, \quad x = 150, \quad x = 5.4, \quad x = -3?$$

It can be seen from the function that x first needs to be multiplied by 2 to give 2x, in order to calculate the different values for f(x). Having done that, 1 is added to achieve the f(x) value. So:

$$x = 1 \qquad f(x) = (2 \times 1) + 1 = 3$$
$$x = 150 \qquad f(x) = (2 \times 150) + 1 = 301$$
$$x = 5.4 \qquad f(x) = (2 \times 5.4) + 1 = 11.8$$
$$x = -3 \qquad f(x) = (2 \times -3) + 1 = -5$$

INVERSE FUNCTIONS

If it costs a school £120 per day for every supply teacher booked, it can clearly be seen that if the school uses 8 supply days in a term it will cost £960. To work out the supply bill, the cost per day is multiplied by the number of days. Suppose the total supply bill is known – to calculate the number of supply days used, the total bill would need to be divided by the cost per day, i.e. $960 \div 120 = 8$. This rule for 'undoing' the original function is called the **inverse function**. The inverse function is often represented as $f^{-1}(x)$.

If this 'undoing' rule is applied to the function from the example above, i.e. $f(x) = 2x + 1$, it is possible to calculate the inverse function.

From this it can be seen that the inverse function is:

$$f^{-1}(x) = \frac{x - 1}{2}$$

What is the relationship between a function and its inverse?

The function $f(x)$ links the number x to the number $f(x)$. The inverse function $f^{-1}(x)$ links $f(x)$ back to x. This can be written as:

$$f^{-1}(f(x)) = x \quad \text{or} \quad f(f^{-1}(x)) = x$$

This can be used to work out inverse functions when finding them by inspection is not easy.

Consider the example $f(x) = 2x + 1$. $f(f^{-1}(x)) = x$ can be used to find the inverse function as follows:

$$f(f^{-1}(x)) = x$$
$$2(f^{-1}(x)) + 1 = x$$
$$2(f^{-1}(x)) = x - 1$$
$$f^{-1}(x) = \frac{x - 1}{2}$$

Points to remember about finding inverse functions:

- **only one-to-one functions have a unique inverse;**
- **the domain of the function is the range of the inverse and the range of the function is the domain of the inverse.**

Graphs

A group of children is investigating circles. From practical activity they have recorded the diameters and circumferences for a range of circles. They use graphing software to produce the following graph:

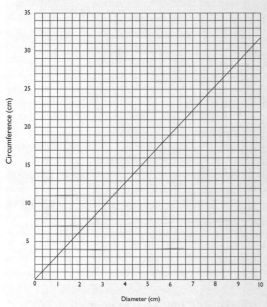

Laura is asked to use the graph to determine the circumference for circles with the following diameters:

(a) 3 cm   (b) 5 cm   (c) 8 cm

She decides the circumferences are:

(a) 10 cm   (b) 15 cm   (c) 25 cm

What does this tell you about her ability to interpret the information represented on the graph?

It can be seen that Laura has simply read the nearest labelled point on the vertical axis and therefore not understood that every point has a meaning. What subject knowledge do you need to be able to extend her understanding of interpreting graphical representation?

For more information on equations, see page 49 for the section on linear and simultaneous equations.

As stated earlier in this chapter, because a linear equation does not involve any powers greater than I, it can always be represented as a straight line graph. Equations involving greater powers of x are curves, e.g.:

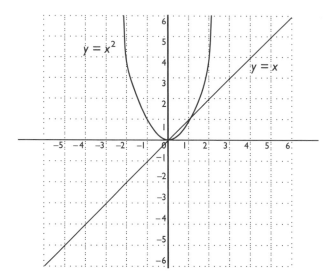

As can be seen from the graph, $y = x$ is a straight line, i.e. **linear**, while $y = x^2$ (a **quadratic** equation) is a curve, in this case a parabola.

But given an equation, how are graphs drawn? And equally, given a graph, how is the equation determined?

Given any linear equation, it is possible to find points which will lie on the line. Taking the equation $y = 3x$, it can be seen that the points $(-2, -6)$, $(0, 0)$, $(1, 3)$, $(1.5, 4.5)$ will all lie on the line. The minimum number of points needed is three – this allows for a check point.

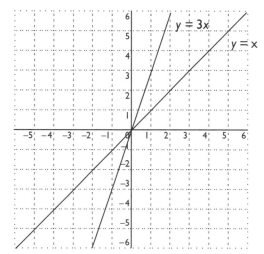

Compare this graph to the graph of $y = x$. It can be seen that they are both straight lines. However they have a different slope or **gradient**.

GRADIENT OF A STRAIGHT LINE

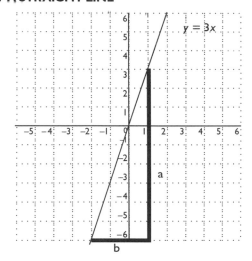

To calculate the gradient of a straight line (often called m), it is necessary to know the co-ordinates of two points. Taking $y = 3x$, the points $(-2, -6)$ and $(1, 3)$ lie on the line. To calculate the gradient the differences must be found between the y co-ordinates (a) and the x co-ordinates (b), then the difference in the y co-ordinates is divided by the difference in the x co-ordinates, i.e. a ÷ b.

$$\text{Gradient (m)} = \frac{a}{b} = \frac{(3 - -6)}{(1 - -2)} = \frac{9}{3} = 3$$

It should be noted at this point that this value is equal to the value that x was multiplied by in the original equation, i.e. $y = 3x$.

So far this chapter has just considered graphs that pass through the origin, i.e. the point $(0,0)$ lies on the graph. But what if a graph does not pass through the origin?

THE Y-INTERCEPT
Consider the graph of the linear function $y = x + 2$.

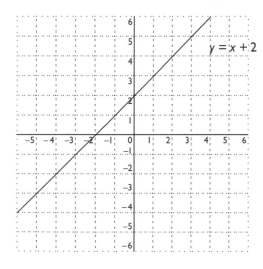

Straightaway it can be seen that the equation of this line differs from those encountered above (i.e. $y = x$ and $y = 3x$). This graph has the equation $y = x + 2$, i.e. something has been added. By looking at the graph of the equation it can be seen that the graph crosses the y-axis at the point (0,2), i.e. when $y = 2$. This is also the value of the number added to the x term in the equation. This number added to the x term is frequently called c.

FINDING EQUATIONS OF GRAPHS

From the above it can be seen that it is possible to find the equation of a graph by calculating the gradient and finding the y-intercept. A linear equation has the general formula:

$$y = mx + c$$

where m is the gradient of the line and c is the y-intercept.

How could the equations of the following lines be found?

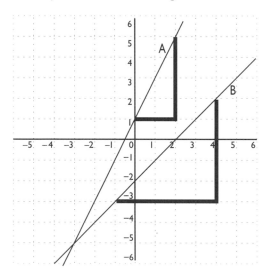

Graph A:

Gradient (m) = 4 ÷ 2 = 2

y-intercept (c) = 1

Substituting these values into the general equation $y = mx + c$ gives:

$y = 2x + 1$

Graph B:

Gradient (m) = 5 ÷ 5 = 1

y-intercept (c) = −2

Substituting these values into the general equation $y = mx + c$ gives:

$y = x - 2$

Equally it is possible to identify the gradient and y-intercept of a graph from the equation of the line, e.g,:

$y = 4x + 3$ has a gradient of 4 and crosses the y-axis at the point (0,3);

$2y = 6x + 1$ has a gradient of 3 (i.e. $6 \div 2$) and a y-intercept of $\frac{1}{2}$ (i.e. $1 \div 2$).

But what happens if the equation is not written in the form $y = mx + c$?

To find the gradient and y-intercept if the equation is not of the form $y = mx + c$ involves rearranging the equation, e.g:

$$
\begin{aligned}
x - 3y &= 6 \\
x &= 6 + 3y \\
x - 6 &= 3y \\
3y &= x - 6 \\
y &= \frac{x}{3} - 2
\end{aligned}
$$

So, the gradient is $\frac{1}{3}$ and the y-intercept is -2.

Algebra, Equations, Functions and Graphs:

a summary of key points

_____ **Terms** *are algebraic quantities that are separated from each other in expressions by + or −.*

_____ **General terms** *can be used to describe sequences.*

_____ **An equation** *is a statement that two expressions are equal.*

_____ **Simultaneous linear equations** *are two linear equations that have a common solution.*

_____ *There is a wide range of methods for solving simultaneous linear equations, including graphing, 'trial and improvement', eliminating unknowns and substitution.*

_____ **Functions** *are rules which change, or map one number onto another.*

_____ *Given a linear equation it is possible to establish the gradient and y-intercept of the graph it represents.*

✓ Self-assessment questions

1 Simplify the following expressions:
(a) $5n^2 + 6n - n^2 + 4 - 2n + 1$ (b) $(pq)^2 + p^2q + 4p^2q^2 - 3p(qp) + pq^2$

2 Find the general term for each of these sequences:

(a)	position	1	2	3	4	5
	term	2	5	8	11	14
(b)	position	1	2	3	4	5
	term	4	8	12	16	20

3 Find the general term for the following sequence:

position (n)	1	2	3	4	5
term	-1	4	11	20	31

4 Solve the following pairs of simultaneous equations:
(a) $a - 3b = 1$ (b) $2a - 3b = 4$
     $a + 2b = 11$ $a + 2b = 9$

5 Find the gradients and the y-intercepts of the graphs of the following equations:
(a) $2y = 6x + 4$ (b) $x + 2y = 4$

Further reading

Deboys, M. and Pitt, E. (1992) *Lines of Development in Primary Mathematics*. Belfast: Blackstaff Press. This book is laid out clearly within mathematical topics and therefore makes referencing very straightforward. It includes sections on number patterns and further number patterns which clearly support algebraic development.

Haylock, D. (2001) *Mathematics Explained for Primary Teachers*. London: Paul Chapman Publishing. As the title suggests, this book explains much of the content of the primary mathematics curriculum. It also addresses key teaching points and gives opportunities to try some self-assessment questions in each area, to further support your subject knowledge development.

Haylock, D. and Cockburn, A. (1997) *Understanding Mathematics in the Lower Primary Years*. London: Paul Chapman Publishing. This book aims to provide readers with a clearer understanding of the mathematics they will encounter in the classroom. Its focuses include mathematical symbolism and developing appropriate mathematical language. It is written for those involved with the teaching of 4- to 8-year-olds.

Hopkins, C., Gifford, S. and Pepperell, S. (1996) *Mathematics in the Primary School: a Sense of Progression*. London: David Fulton. The title of this book clearly states the content which is a progression in mathematics. It includes a section entitled 'From pattern to algebra' which details the progression in developing algebraic understanding.

Williams, E. and Shuard, H. (1997) *Primary Mathematics Today*. Harlow: Longman. This book is an extremely comprehensive text covering all aspects of primary mathematics, including aspects of graphing. It supports subject knowledge development very effectively, while at the same time considering pedagogical issues and clearly detailing progression.

Introduction

Measurements are used throughout the world by people wishing to determine the physical features of an object such as its length or **mass**, or to chart the passing of time. When children wish to measure they must first have acquired the language needed to describe the experience. Through discussion with peers, teacher, parents they will have been exposed to the use of appropriate language for measures such as longer, shorter, heavier and wider. Children will have compared sizes such as pieces of birthday cake, bags of sweets, towers of bricks without having had the need to count. They will have used intuition and estimation skills for measuring before using arbitrary units such as shells and conkers. The understanding of the need for non-standard units such as cubes and cotton reels will have followed and finally the realisation that standard units such as metres, centimetres, kilograms are necessary in everyday life where the relationship of one measure to another is what is important.

Professional Standards for QTS

 ### 2.1b

To achieve QTS you need to have a secure knowledge and understanding of the mathematics content of the National Curriculum for Key Stages 1 and 2 and the methods and expectations set out in the National Numeracy Strategy. For measures this includes:

- *that the basis of measures is exact and that practical measurement is approximate;*
- *standard measures and compound measures, including rates of change;*
- *the relationship between measures, including length, area, volume and capacity;*
- *the importance of choice of unit and use of proportion.*

You may find it helpful to read through the appropriate section of the Handbook that accompanies the Standards for the award of QTS for clarification and support.

Curriculum Guidance for the Foundation Stage, the National Curriculum and the National Numeracy Strategy

The Curriculum Guidance for the Foundation Stage recognises the importance of certain key skills in mathematical development. By the end of the foundation stage most children will be able to use language such as 'more' or 'less', 'greater' or 'smaller', 'heavier' or 'lighter', to compare two numbers or quantities, and use developing mathematical ideas and methods to solve practical problems.

Within the National Curriculum for mathematics at Key Stage 1, pupils should be taught to estimate the size of objects and order them by direct comparison using appropriate language; put familiar events in chronological order; compare and measure objects using uniform non-standard units (straws, wooden cubes), then with a standard unit of length (cm, m), mass (kg), capacity (l); compare the duration of events using a standard unit of time; understand angle as a measure of turn using whole turns, half turns, and quarter turns; estimate, measure and weigh objects; choose and use simple measuring instruments, reading and interpreting numbers and scales to the nearest labelled division.

At Key Stage 2, pupils should be taught to recognise the need for standard units of length, mass and capacity, choose which ones are suitable for a task, and use them to make sensible estimates in everyday situations; convert one metric unit to another (3.17 kg to 3170 g); know the rough metric equivalents of imperial units still in daily use; recognise that measures are approximate; choose and use suitable measuring instruments for a task; interpret numbers and read scales with increasing accuracy; record measurements using decimal notation; recognise angles as greater or less than a right angle or half turn, estimate their size and order them; measure and draw acute, obtuse and right angles to the nearest degree; read the time from analogue and digital 12 and 24 hour clocks; use units of time — seconds, minutes, hours, days, weeks — and know the relationship between them; find perimeters of simple shapes; find areas of rectangles using the formula, understanding its connection to counting squares and how it extends this approach; calculate the perimeter and area of shapes composed of rectangles.

The National Numeracy Strategy's *Framework* has five strands of which measures is the fourth. Using and applying mathematics is integrated throughout the strands. The measures strand includes choosing units and reading scales and the properties of 2-D and 3-D shapes, position, direction and movement. It also includes the more specific topics of measurement of length, mass, capacity, perimeter, area, time, direction and angle.

The *Framework* emphasises the importance of the integration of using and applying mathematics and gives the following examples: making and justifying decisions about methods, equipment or units of measure; describing properties of shapes or numbers and reasoning about them; explaining methods of calculation; devising and refining methods of recording calculations; checking results.

Stages of development

The following three stages are important in the teaching and learning of measures. It is important for your own subject knowledge that you understand the various stages and the associated vocabulary. The activities suggested here are merely examples to aid your understanding of the concept, although most have been used in school.

Direct comparison using matching, with no actual measuring

Practical activities such as comparing the size of daddy bear's and mummy bear's bowls, the length of Sally's and Jenny's hair, the mass of a bottle and a carton of juice are important at this stage for encouraging the development of language and mathematical vocabulary.

RESEARCH SUMMARY

The main tool for child and teacher to employ in the mastery of maths concepts is language, not pencil and paper exercises from textbooks. The child is encouraged to talk about what she is doing and the teacher's craft is to bring all her knowledge and skill into play to make her intervention appropriate (Sue Atkinson, 1992).

Piaget has shown that this intuitive judgment of comparison is the earliest step towards measuring. By comparing two lengths and asking questions such as 'how much longer?' we are introducing the concept of difference which will lead to a better understanding of subtraction later on. In addition, by introducing the idea of 'how many times as long?' we are paving the way to a better understanding of ratio and division.

RESEARCH SUMMARY

'At the secondary level proportionality is one of the most researched areas of mathematics, not only in Britain but around the world. The universal conclusion is that children on the whole find metric (to do with measurements) proportionality very difficult but, more importantly, this research has thrown light on the misconceptions and errors which affect performance' (Frobisher, et al., 1999).

Using non-standard units

Children in practical activities will use non-standard units such as shells, cupfuls, pebbles, beans, conkers, cubes and bricks. They need lots of experience with real-life objects and measuring length, area, volume, capacity and mass before they can begin to understand the concept of **conservation**. For example, if a piece of paper is torn in two or three pieces, does the surface area remain the same? If I break a ball of plasticine into three smaller balls do I still have the same mass of plasticine?

Standard units

Having had experience in using non-standard units, children will begin to see the need for standard units. They will realise that by using non-standard units to compare the lengths, masses and volumes of objects their results may be unreliable and inconsistent. It is important that the skill of **estimation** is developed at this stage and that children should always be encouraged to offer an estimate before carrying out an activity. Your classroom should be a comfortable environment where children are encouraged to take risks without fear of ridicule if they provide a 'wrong' answer. Children who are freed from the fear of criticism will more readily experiment with ideas and mathematical language. Estimating before a practical activity helps to dispel the belief that some children may have of mathematics – 'it is either right or wrong'. What is fundamentally important is that the process is more important than the product at this stage. A useful resource, which helps reinforce this skill, is an 'estimating table'. This could be an area of the classroom which has a small selection of everyday items on it such as a medium-sized apple, a packet of rich tea biscuits, a can of coke, a bag a sugar. Children could hold these items using their hand as a balance and write down their estimate of mass before posting it in a box on the display. At a certain time during the week the teacher could open the box and read out the estimates before weighing the items and discussing the outcomes. This also has the benefit of helping the children to remember certain masses, and so when faced with an item whose mass they are unsure of, they can compare it with an item already known. For example, I know that a bag of sugar has a mass of 1 kg/2.2 lbs so I can use that knowledge to work out the mass of another item I am unsure of.

Understanding units and measures

The standard units of measures you'll need to know are set out below, followed by *approximate* equivalences:

	Metric	Imperial		Metric	Imperial
Mass	g, kg, tonnes	ounces, pounds, stones	Mass	25 g	1 oz
				1 kg	2.2 lb
Volume	cm^3, m^3	cubic inches/feet		50 kg	8 stones
				1 tonne	1 ton
Capacity	ml, cl, litre	fluid ounces, pints, gallons	Volume	16 cm^3	1 cubic inch
				1 m^3	37 cubic feet
Length	cm, m, km	inches, feet, yards, miles	Capacity	570 ml	1 pint
				1 litre	1.75 pints
Area	cm^2, m^2, hectares	square inches/feet/yards		5 litres	1 gallon
			Length	2.5 cm	1 inch
Time		seconds, minutes, hours		30 cm	1 foot
				1 m	39 inches
				8 km	5 miles
			Area	6 cm^2	1 square inch
				1 m^2	11 square feet

Although in Britain today we still refer to **imperial measures** (introduced in the Magna Carta in 1215) such as pints, gallons and miles on a daily basis, the metric system is widely recognised as being the most commonly used system for measuring. The **Système International**, or **S.I.**, determines the units of measurement used in the metric system. They include:

- **millimetres, centimetres, metres, kilometres – length, area;**
- **grams, kilograms – mass;**
- **seconds, minutes, hours – time;**
- **millilitres, litres – capacity;**
- **cubic centimetres – volume;**
- **degrees – angles.**

Knowledge and understanding

Mass and weight

Think about this

Akeva weighs a ball of plasticine and says it has a mass of 150 g. He then breaks up the ball into a number of pieces and says it will have a greater mass because there are more pieces. What subject knowledge do you need to effectively support and develop Akeva's understanding of mass and weight?

To begin with it is necessary to understand the difference between mass and weight. These terms are commonly misused In the primary classroom where children often refer to the 'mass' of an object as its 'weight', e.g. when using a balance we put an object in one pan and balance it with 500 grams. The object does not weigh 500 grams – it is equal to the weight of the 500 gram mass or its mass is 500 grams. The mass is the quantity of matter in an object and the weight is a force that depends on gravity. When faced with the concept of mass, the problem we have is that we cannot directly see or feel the amount of mass in an object. When we hold something in our hand it is the force we are using which determines how heavy the object feels and it is this force which reduces as we move further from the centre of the earth. If we were to hold the same object while standing on the moon we would discover that its weight had changed dramatically but its mass would remain unchanged. We know that when the gravitational pull of an astronaut in space is less than that on earth, then he can experience weightlessness.

Children come to school with a wide experience of mass and weight. For example, they have weighed out ingredients for baking a cake; they have heard discussions at home about dieting and losing 'weight'; they have seen vegetables and fruit being weighed in the supermarket, and cheese and ham being weighed in the deli and therefore, understandably, find difficulty when faced with a new word which deals with the concept of weight as they know it. When weighing an amount of cheese we say it is 250 grams. What we mean is that its weight is equal to a 250-gram mass and that its mass is 250 grams. If we wish to lose weight ourselves then it's a trip to the moon we need! We can weigh 60 kg on our bathroom scales at home here on earth but were we to take these scales and weigh ourselves on the moon, we would find that we weighed a mere sixth of our weight on earth – 10 kg! We do not lose weight when we diet; we lose some of our mass.

In order to implement this language in the classroom we need to make the distinction between units of weight, which are newtons, and units of mass, which are grams and kilograms. By referring to these units correctly and labelling equipment used with the balance scales as 50-g masses, 100-gram masses, etc., we are one step nearer to clarifying the distinction between mass and weight.

Volume and capacity

Think about this

Having filled a saucepan with water and then placed a number of large potatoes in it, Joe notices that the water begins to overflow. He suggests that if he chops up the potatoes into smaller pieces the water will not rise as much. What knowledge do you need in order to move Joe's learning on?

According to Archimedes' principle, a body partially or wholly submerged in liquid experiences an upward force equal to the weight of fluid it displaces.

As with mass and weight, it is important that the distinction between the meaning of **volume** and the meaning of **capacity** is made. When we talk about volume we mean the amount of three-dimensional space something occupies and we normally measure this in cubic units. Capacity, on the other hand, refers to the actual container and describes how much liquid volume it can hold when full. Capacity is measured in millilitres or litres.

Practical task

How many different shaped boxes with a volume of 20 cubic centimetres can you find?

Archimedes told us how to find the volume of our hand by placing it in a container full of water and measuring the amount of water that has been displaced by it. Pour the amount of displaced water into a measuring jug and then convert the amount of millilitres you have displaced into cubic centimetres.

Investigating Archimedes' principle of water displacement will further enhance your knowledge and understanding of the links between cubic centimetres and millilitres.

Practical task

Try placing a variety of irregular shaped objects in a cylinder of water. Take note of the level of the water in the cylinder before you start and watch how the water line is raised when you place the object in the container. By how much did the level of the water increase? You can now find the difference between the original level of water in the container and the higher level. Convert your millilitres to cubic centimetres and you will have found the volume of an irregular shape.

Finding volumes of regular shapes can be done by filling the shape with cubic centimetres. You will begin to notice that the number of cubic centimetres you need to cover the base will tell you the area of the base. Count how many cubic centimetres high your container is. If you multiply the area of the base of your container by its height your answer should be equivalent to the number of cubes you have in your container (see below). By carrying out these activities you are demonstrating the links between the measurement of volume and capacity.

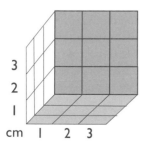

Finding the volume
of a regular shape

The discovery that I litre of water has the same volume as 1000 cubic centimetres is a very important one. Through further investigation, children will also discover the relationship between millilitres, cubic centimetres and grams. The mass of I kilogram of water is equivalent to I litre or 1000 cubic centimetres.

- **The volume of a cube/cuboid is given by length × breadth × height (l × b × h).**

VOLUME OF PRISMS

Having found the volume of cubes and cuboids by filling them with centimetre cubes, then by using the formula of area of base times height, we can now work out the volume of half a cube or cuboid. Knowing that making a diagonal cut through a

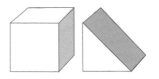

cube yields two identical triangular prisms should help you to understand that each of these triangular prisms will have the volume of half a cube. The bases of the prisms are right-angled triangles, whose area will be half that of the square face of the cube. By multiplying the area of the base of the prism by its height we can find the volume of a triangular prism.

- **The volume of a triangular prism is half (length × breadth × height) $\frac{1}{2}(l \times b \times h)$.**

CONES AND CYLINDERS

How can we find the volume of a cone? Is there any relationship between the volume of a cone and the volume of a cylinder? In order to find out about the relationship we can refer to Archimedes' displacement principle again and immerse a cone and cylinder of equal height and radius in containers of liquid. By doing this a number of times with different sized cones and cylinders we will begin to see a pattern in our results. We will discover that the volume of a cone is approximately one third of the volume of a cylinder. To check our results, we could see if there was the same pattern when measuring the capacity of both the cone and cylinder. By making the cone and cylinder out of card and filling them with sand, we should see that it takes three times as much sand to fill the cylinder.

- **The volume of a cylinder is given by $\pi r^2 h$.**
- **The volume of a cone is given by $\frac{1}{3}\pi r^2 h$.**

Practical task

Use three pieces of card which are equal in size. Make a cylinder, cuboid and triangular prism. Predict which container will have the greatest volume. Fill them with sand. Which holds the most sand? Why?

Surface area

 For more information on polyhedra, see page 92 for the section on surface area and volume.

The surface area of a **polyhedron** is equal to the sum of the area of its faces. To calculate the surface area of a cube you simply need to know the length of one **edge** (L). From this it is possible to calculate the area of each face (L x L) and multiply it by the number of faces – in this case 6. This will give you the answer $6L^2$. For a cuboid it is necessary to know the length, breadth and height in order to be able to calculate the area of each face and thus the overall surface area.

To calculate the surface area of a cylinder it is necessary to calculate the areas of the two circular faces and then to calculate the area of the curved face which, if rolled out, you will realise is actually a rectangle.

Remember!

- **Area of a circle = πr^2.**
- **Circumference of a circle = $2\pi r$.**

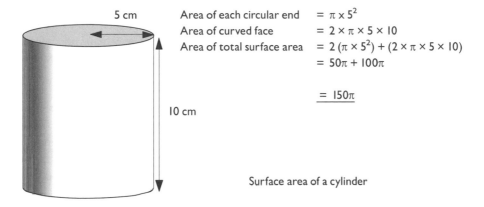

Area of each circular end	$= \pi \times 5^2$
Area of curved face	$= 2 \times \pi \times 5 \times 10$
Area of total surface area	$= 2\,(\pi \times 5^2) + (2 \times \pi \times 5 \times 10)$
	$= 50\pi + 100\pi$
	$\underline{= 150\pi}$

Surface area of a cylinder

Time

Think about this

You ask one of your pupils, Julie, this question: if we leave for our holiday at 09:43 hours and arrive at our destination at 13:15 hours, how long did our journey take?

Julie answers 3 hours 72 minutes and shows you her method:

$$
\begin{array}{r}
13:15 \\
-\ 09:43 \\
\hline
03:72
\end{array}
$$

Is this method appropriate?

RESEARCH SUMMARY

'Because time is one aspect of measurement that has not gone metric the relationships between the units are particularly challenging' (Haylock, 2001).

There are two aspects of time which children need to understand. Firstly there is the interval of time. For example, the time between morning play and lunchtime; the time between my birthday and yours; the time between Easter and summer. These intervals are measured in seconds, minutes, days, weeks, months, years, decades, etc. Children use their memory and important events which provide landmarks to understand the passing of time. The second aspect of time is recorded time. This is the time that something happens. We use analogue or digital time and the date to say exactly when an event occurred. An example of this might be:

'The school concert will take place on Saturday 26 October 2002 at 7:30p.m.'

For more information on complementary addition, see page 13 in the number chapter.

If we were to state that the expected finishing time of the concert was 10p.m. then we could work out the interval of time between the start and the finish as being two and a half hours. When calculating the time interval between two times, using a standard written algorithm is not recommended. The method known as 'shopkeeper's addition' is the most useful way of calculating the difference between two times. Start with 7:30 and work out how many minutes till 8:00 (30). Now work out how many hours from 8:00 until 10:00 (2). Add your results together and you will get two and a half hours or two hours 30 minutes.

THE 24 HOUR CLOCK

As this system is now used for rail, air, bus and boat timetables as well as video recorders, microwaves and watches, you will need to be familiar with it and its relationship with the 12 hour clock. The following diagram is from Deboys and Pitt (1979) and is a useful device for highlighting the relationships between analogue and digital time.

In this system we always use 4 digits to express the time. We use the first two digits for the hours and the last two for the minutes. You must be aware of the distinction between how we 'say' the time and how we 'say' decimal numbers. When we wish to say the time is 13:30, we say: 'The time is thirteen thirty'. However, to express this as a decimal number we would say: 'Thirteen point three' and not 'thirteen point thirty'.

Beware also of the colloquial use of 'fifteen hundred' which is used to express the time 15:00. It suggests that the presence of two zeros means a hundred, which is a common misunderstanding amongst pupils.

Because time is non-metric, children need to learn that bridging through 10 or 100 is not always appropriate. A digital clock displaying 7:59 will in two minutes display 8:01 not 7:61. When working with minutes and hours it is necessary to bridge through 60 and with hours and days through 24. Digital clocks could suggest to children that minutes behave like ordinary numbers and so they might count on 59, 60, 61, not realising that when 60 is reached they have reached a new hour and must go back to zero with their counting. It is important therefore that you plan activities and discussion around this potential misconception. Reference to the clock face should help children see why this form of counting is not appropriate under these circumstances.

Practical task

The ferry leaves the island at 9:43. It reaches the mainland at 13:15. How long is the journey from the island to the mainland?

To calculate the difference, start with 9:43 and count on to 10:00. How many minutes have you counted on? (17) From 10:00 to 13:00 it is another 3 hours. So far we have 3 hours and 17 minutes. From 13:00 hours to 13:15 is another 15 minutes. Added together we have 3 hours, 17 minutes and 15 minutes. This makes 3 hours 32 minutes altogether. Written as a standard algorithm this calculation would be cumbersome and open to misconceptions. It may look like this:

```
   0  12  1
  13:15
-  9:43
  3:72
```

A.M. AND P.M.

a.m. is an abbreviation for ante-meridian, meaning before noon, and p.m. is an abbreviation for post-meridian, meaning after noon. This means that 12 noon is neither a.m. nor p.m. and similarly that 12 midnight is neither a.m. nor p.m. We say 12 noon or 12 midnight when we wish to make the distinction between them. In the 24 hour system the time one minute after 23:59 is not 24:00 but 00:00, the beginning of a new day, and we call this 'zero hours'. However, when the time is zero hours it does not mean that time has disappeared. Likewise, when the thermometer reads zero degrees there is still a temperature that we can feel. This is the main distinction between a **ratio scale** and an **interval scale**. In a ratio scale, the zero means nothing, e.g. a length of zero metres is no length, a mass of zero grams is nothing, and a bottle containing zero millilitres is empty!

INTERVAL SCALE

Comparing two times gives us the difference in time between the two. It does not tell us that 2 o'clock is three times less than 6 o'clock. It tells us that 2 o'clock is 4 hours earlier than 6 o'clock. This is an example of an interval scale. Similarly when comparing two temperatures we cannot say, because it is 15 degrees here and 45 degrees else-where, that it is three times hotter in the other place!

ANGLES

An **angle** is simply a way of describing a measurement of turn. We call its unit of measurement the degree. When two lines meet at a right angle (90°) we call them **perpendicular lines**.

On the other hand, two lines which travel in the same direction but which never meet are called **parallel lines**.

When two straight lines intersect each other, the two angles that lie opposite each other are called **vertically opposite angles**.

Since the lines that are intersecting are straight lines, their angles must add up to 180°. We call the angles that are adjacent to each other on the straight line **supplementary angles**.

Where parallel lines are crossed by a straight line, we not only create vertically opposite angles but also **corresponding angles** which are equal:

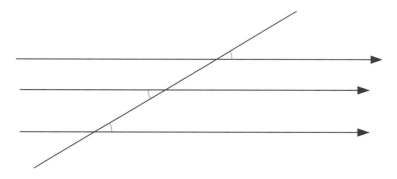

C For more information on the properties and angles of shape, see pages 77–83 of the chapter on shape and space.

The angles marked in this diagram are alternate angles which are also equal.

We can study the concept of angle in two different ways. The first is what we call a 'static' experience. This involves comparing angles with what we know already. For instance, we can look at an angle and decide whether or not it is greater or smaller than a right angle. We can look for the difference in the shape made by two lines or for the difference in direction between the two lines.

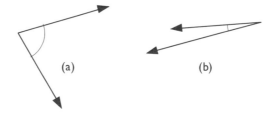

(a)   (b)

The angle marked in (a) is greater than the angle in (b). The difference in the shape made by the two sets of lines is obvious because of the difference in the direction of the lines.

The second experience we can have when studying the concept of angle is a 'dynamic' experience. This is the preferable option as it lends itself to a more practical approach leading to greater understanding of the concept. For instance, by slowly opening a book we can see the angle between the pages growing as the book opens wider. Similarly if we open and close a door slowly we can see the size of the angle changing.

Using two geostrips joined together at one end can create a worthwhile visual and practical experience when we gradually open the strips wider and wider. Playing games which involve turning ourselves in different directions is another example of dynamic geometry. Obviously we must ensure that we understand the link between static and dynamic geometry so that when faced with a 2-D representation we can visualise the rotation involved and understand the measurement of turn.

The instruments we use to measure angles are protractors and angle measurers. The most useful protractor in primary school is the 360° angle measurer which emphasises the dynamic view of the angle.

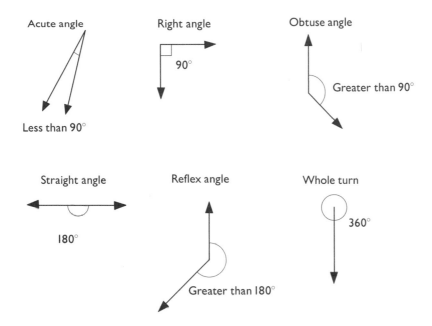

Bearings and compass points

A bearing indicates the direction of one point in relation to another point. It is measured from a line which points due North in a clockwise direction and is always given as a three digit number.

y has a bearing of 045° from x.   y has a bearing of 240° from x.

Measures:

a summary of key points

____ *Estimation and approximation are fundamental to measuring.*

____ *Discovery through practical work is essential for the understanding of measures, e.g. while working with shape and space, include calculating and measuring length, area, volume and capacity to demonstrate your knowledge and understanding of compound measures.*

____ *The dynamic view of angle is fundamental to understanding the concept of angle.*

____ *Acknowledge the incorrect use of 'weight' in daily use, while striving to use the correct terminology of 'mass'.*

____ *Understand the relationship between measures, e.g. cubic centimetres and millilitres, and know that 1 kg = 1l = 1000 cubic centimetres.*

✓ Self-assessment questions

1 *The weight of an average man is 72 kg. What will it be on the moon?*

2 *The volume of a box is 400 cubic centimetres. What is its capacity?*

3 *Draw a transitivity diagram which demonstrates relationships between (a) lengths (b) volumes (c) times.*

4 *Put these angles in order, draw them and classify them as acute, obtuse, or reflex: 212°, 62°, 87°, 134°, $\frac{1}{4}$ turn, $\frac{7}{8}$ of a turn, 23°.*

Transitive property is explained on page 31 in the number chapter.

Further reading

Deboys, M. and Pitt, E. (1992) *Lines of Development in Primary Mathematics*. Belfast: Blackstaff Press. The layout of this book makes for easily accessible topics and therefore is useful for referencing purposes. The activities featured in the measures sections will provide children with essential, worthwhile and valuable practical experiences.

Haylock, Derek (2001) *Mathematics Explained For Primary Teachers*. London: Paul Chapman. This book is essential reading for primary teachers who wish to increase their confidence in mathematics. The chapter on measures clearly defines the principles which are central to teaching measurement in the primary school.

Hopkins, C., Gifford, S. and Pepperell, S. (1996). *Mathematics in the Primary School*. London: David Fulton. Measures chapter features a helpful guide in relation to metric/imperial measures and equivalences.

Williams, E. M. and Shuard, H. (1997) *Primary Mathematics Today*. Harlow: Longman. An extremely comprehensive text covering all aspects of primary mathematics. It supports subject knowledge while considering pedagogical issues clearly.

Introduction

An understanding of shape and space is vital to us as people who live in and move around a three-dimensional world. As we attempt to make sense of that world we develop visual images and vocabulary to support our developing spatial understanding. We represent our 3-D environment within 2-D media, e.g. pictures and text, and we use language to describe our position and movements. Understanding geometry is therefore crucial as we explore and extend our understanding of shape, space and movement.

Professional Standards for QTS

 2.1b

To achieve QTS you need to have a secure knowledge and understanding of the mathematics content of the National Curriculum for Key Stages 1 and 2 and the methods and expectations set out in the National Numeracy Strategy. For shape and space this includes:

- *Cartesian co-ordinates in 2-D;*
- *2-D transformations;*
- *angles, congruence and similarity in triangles and other shapes;*
- *geometrical constructions;*
- *identifying and measuring properties and characteristics of 2-D shapes;*
- *using Pythagoras' theorem;*
- *recognising the relationships between and using the formulae for the area of 2-D shapes, including rectangle and triangle, trapezium, and parallelogram;*
- *the calculation of the area of circles and sectors, the length of circumferences and arcs;*
- *recognise, understand and use formulae for the surface area and volume of prisms;*
- *identifying 3-D solids and shapes and recognising their properties and characteristics.*

You may find it helpful to read through the appropriate section of the Handbook that accompanies the Standards for the award of QTS for clarification and support.

Curriculum Guidance for the Foundation Stage, the National Curriculum and the National Numeracy Strategy

The Curriculum Guidance for the Foundation Stage recognises the importance of certain key skills in mathematical development. The areas of learning identified include working with shape and space. This links clearly to the NNS Key Objectives for Reception: use language such as circle or bigger to describe the shape and size of solids and flat shapes; use everyday language to describe position.

Within the Mathematics National Curriculum the Programmes of Study clearly state the knowledge, skills and understanding which are to be taught throughout the Key Stages. These are closely linked to the Key Objectives identified for each year group with the NNS *Framework for Teaching Mathematics*.

At both Key Stage 1 and 2, children need to be able to describe the properties of 2-D and 3-D shapes. They need to be able to name and describe a growing range of shapes, as well as identifying their symmetries. The children need to develop an understanding of position in space by studying 2-D transformations as well as co-ordinates in four quadrants. There is an emphasis on developing correct mathematical vocabulary to talk about spatial concepts. All of these aspects are clearly reflected within the NNS Key Objectives for Years 1 to 6.

RESEARCH SUMMARY

Fuys, Geddes and Tischler (1988) in Clements et al. (1999) emphasise the importance of introducing children to geometric problems in the early years of schooling. This should include encountering shapes in different orientations and the classification of shapes. They warn that if this does not take place it could result in 'geometrically deprived' children.

Battista (1999) identifies 'spatial structuring' as a key operation to understanding spatial concepts. Spatial structuring is defined as the 'mental operation of constructing an organisation or form for an object or set of objects'. Spatial structuring is then used to determine the nature, shape or composition by identifying spatial components. We associate and combine components to establish interrelationships. Studying shape and space involves the structuring and analysis of space. We structure space when we describe it in terms of lines, angles, polygons, polyhedra, etc. and when we transform shapes. Children need to develop spatial structuring in order to structure what is, for them, an unstructured world.

Both of these findings are reiterated by Anne Cockburn (1999) when she describes some of the intrinsic problems children face when learning about shape. 2-D and 3-D shapes look different depending on the angle from which they are viewed. This, coupled with the fact that many school texts represent 2-D shapes with a particular orientation (usually one straight edge is parallel to the bottom of the page), results in children failing to recognise the same shapes with different orientation, e.g. they call a square at 45° to the bottom of the page a diamond. There are also problems associated with how children perceive shapes. This links to Battista's 'spatial structuring'. We cannot assume that the features forming the focus of the child's attention are similar to our own when perceiving figures or dividing figures. Children may focus on different aspects of the situation. Triadafillidis (1995) (in Cockburn, 1999) found that haptic exploration (i.e. handling shapes without seeing them, e.g. in 'feely bags') helped children to recognise shapes later presented visually. This also supported a recognition of 2-D representations of 3-D shapes.

Knowledge and understanding

Polygons

A child, Alex, is asked to name the following shapes and then identify the numbers of lines of reflective symmetry and the orders of rotational symmetry.

Shape 1   Shape 2

Alex decides the following:

- *Shape 1 is an octagon. It has 16 lines of reflective symmetry and rotational symmetry of order 9.*
- *Shape 2 is a star. It has 8 lines of reflective symmetry and rotational symmetry of order 5.*

What does this tell you about his understanding of polygons?

It is clear that Alex solely associates the polygon names with regular polygons and not with irregular ones. What knowledge do you need to be able to effectively support and extend his understanding of naming polygons?

NAMING POLYGONS

Polygon comes from the Greek — *poly* meaning 'many' and *gon* from '*gonu*' meaning 'knee'. So a polygon is a shape with many knees!

It would be possible to keep naming polygons indefinitely and scholars have worked out systems to keep naming polygons up to those with millions of sides. However, within primary mathematics it is more usual to deal with polygons up to a dodecagon (12 sides).

3 sides: triangle (also sometimes referred to as a trigon for mathematical consistency)

4 sides: quadrilateral (also sometimes referred to as a tetragon for mathematical consistency)

5 sides: pentagon

6 sides: hexagon

7 sides: heptagon

8 sides: octagon

9 sides: enneagon (frequently referred to as a nonagon)

10 sides: decagon

11 sides: hendecagon

12 sides: dodecagon

If you are interested in finding out more about naming polygons with a greater number of sides there are plenty of websites containing this information.

REGULAR OR IRREGULAR?

From the responses it is clear that Alex did not understand the concept of regular and irregular polygons. If a polygon is regular this indicates that all its sides are of equal length and all the interior angles are the same size. If it is irregular then its sides are not of the same length, nor are its interior angles all the same size. Thus, the 'star' identified by Alex is an irregular octagon.

REFLECTIVE SYMMETRY

Alex was not successful in identifying the number of lines of reflective symmetry.

A shape is said to have reflective or line symmetry if you can fold it so that one half fits exactly on top of the other half. The line through the middle, the line of symmetry, is like a mirror; each half is a reflection of the other.

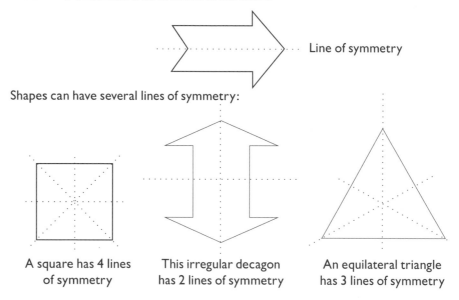

Line of symmetry

Shapes can have several lines of symmetry:

A square has 4 lines of symmetry

This irregular decagon has 2 lines of symmetry

An equilateral triangle has 3 lines of symmetry

A regular polygon has the same number of lines of symmetry as number of sides.

Alex correctly identified the lines of symmetry but counted them incorrectly. By counting around the octagon he counted both ends of each line and thus counted every line twice, ending up with an answer twice that of the correct answer.

ROTATIONAL SYMMETRY

Alex was not successful in identifying the orders of rotational symmetry.

A shape is said to have rotational symmetry if it looks the same in different positions when rotated about its centre.

(In these diagrams the spot is there to help identify the order of rotational symmetry and should not be considered as part of the square.)

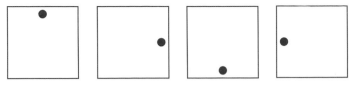

Rotational symmetry

It can be seen that, in each of the four positions above, the square looks exactly the same. So, the order of rotational symmetry of the square is 4.

Try this with a rectangle (use a book or a piece of A4 paper) and you will notice that a rectangle has rotational symmetry of order 2.

What do you notice about regular polygons? A regular polygon has an order of rotational symmetry equal to the number of sides.

Any shape, however strange, will have rotational symmetry of order 1, since there is one position where it looks the same!

Alex understood that in order to identify the order of rotation it was necessary to rotate about a point. However, he then counted the starting position twice, once at the beginning and again at the end of the count. Therefore the answer in both cases was 1 greater than the correct order.

Triangles

Unlike many other polygons, different kinds of triangles have different names. Thus it is possible to give specific names to irregular triangles based on their particular properties (below).

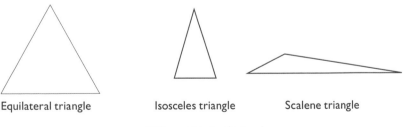

Equilateral triangle   Isosceles triangle   Scalene triangle

Different kinds of triangle

A regular triangle is called an **equilateral triangle**. Because it is a regular polygon it is clear that all the sides must be of equal length and all the interior angles must be the same size (60°). Again, because an equilateral triangle is regular, it must also have 3 lines of reflective symmetry and rotational symmetry of order 3.

A triangle which has 2 sides of equal length is called an **isosceles triangle**. As well as having two sides of equal length, an isosceles triangle also has two angles of equal size. An isosceles triangle has 1 line of reflective symmetry and rotational symmetry of order 1. The name isosceles derives from the Greek *iso* (same) and *skelos* (leg).

A triangle which has three sides of different length and no equal angles is called a **scalene triangle**. Scalene triangles have no lines of reflective symmetry and rotational symmetry of order 1.

A triangle containing one angle of 90° is called a right-angled triangle. A right-angled triangle will also be either isosceles or scalene.

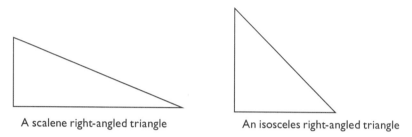

A scalene right-angled triangle   An isosceles right-angled triangle

Right-angled triangles

The number of lines of reflective symmetry of a right-angled triangle depend upon whether it is isosceles or scalene.

The right-angled triangle is also a special shape as it is possible to use Pythagoras' theorem to calculate the length of the longest side.

PYTHAGORAS' THEOREM

Pythagoras (582–507 BCE) was a Greek philosopher and geometrician. He founded the Pythagorean Brotherhood, a secretive group who refused to share their mathematical discoveries. It all back-fired in a rather unpleasant way when, owing to the suspicion and fear of the locals, and encouraged by a rival of Pythagoras, many of the Brotherhood, including their leader, were killed when their buildings were set alight.

Pythagoras' theorem states that it is possible to calculate the length of the longest side (the hypotenuse) of a right-angled triangle by finding the square root of the sum of the squares of the other two sides of the triangle. In some right-angled triangles it is very simple to work out the length of the hypotenuse because all the numbers work out as whole numbers. If a triangle has two sides one of 3 cm and the other of 4 cm, what is the length of the hypotenuse?

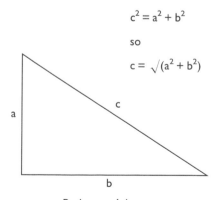

$$c^2 = a^2 + b^2$$

so

$$c = \sqrt{(a^2 + b^2)}$$

Pythagoras' theorem

$$c = \sqrt{(9 + 16)}$$
$$c = \sqrt{25}$$
$$c = 5$$

So the hypotenuse is 5 cm long.

This will also be true for multiples of these numbers, e.g.:

if a = 6 and b = 8 then c = 10 because 36 + 64 = 100.

Another set of numbers which are easy to calculate are a = 5 and b = 12. What is the length of the hypotenuse here?

$$c = \sqrt{(25 + 144)}$$
$$c = \sqrt{169}$$
$$c = 13$$

So the hypotenuse is 13 cm long.

Sets of three whole numbers that perfectly fit Pythagoras' equation are called Pythagorean triples.

How does this work? The following diagrams show how Pythagoras' theorem works.

Taking the 3 cm, 4 cm, 5 cm right-angled triangle the following can be seen:

 + =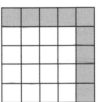

From this it is clear that $3^2 + 4^2 = 5^2$.

The following diagram illustrates how this can be shown, starting with any right-angled triangle:

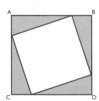

The square in the middle of the four triangles is the square on the hypotenuse of any of these triangles.

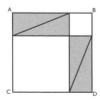

The square ABCD remains unchanged. By moving the four triangles it is possible to create two squares instead of one. These two squares are on the other two sides of the triangle. Because the area of ABCD remains unchanged the sum of the areas of the two smaller squares must be equal to the area of the square on the hypotenuse.

Quadrilaterals

Just as with triangles, irregular quadrilaterals can also be named. Again, the names depend on the properties of the particular quadrilateral.

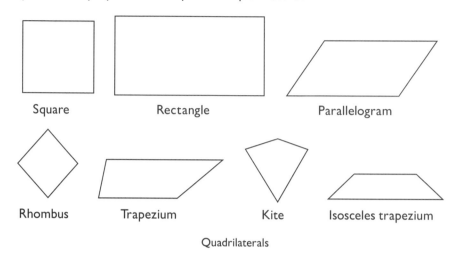

Quadrilaterals

A regular quadrilateral is called a **square**. Because it is a regular polygon it is clear that all the sides must be of equal length and all the interior angles must be the same size (90°). The diagonals of a square are equal in length and bisect each other (i.e. cut each other in half) at right angles. Because a square is regular it must also have 4 lines of reflective symmetry and rotational symmetry of order 4.

A **rectangle** has four right angles, the opposite sides are of equal length and parallel. The diagonals are also equal in length and bisect each other. Rectangles have at least 2 lines of reflective symmetry and rotational symmetry of order 2. Why 'at least'? Because a square has all the characteristics required of a rectangle − it has four right angles, the opposite sides are equal in length and parallel and the diagonals are equal in length and bisect each other. Thus a square also falls into the rectangle category, but has 4 lines of symmetry and rotational symmetry of order 4, hence the 'at least'.

When is a rectangle not a square? When it is an **oblong**! An oblong is a 2-D shape that can be described as 'a rectangle which is not a square'.

A **parallelogram** has opposite sides that are equal in length and parallel and the opposite angles are of equal size. The diagonals bisect each other. Parallelograms have at least a rotational symmetry of order 2. Again it is 'at least' because there are some special cases which fit the description of a parallelogram but have different symmetry properties.

Are the square and the rectangle parallelograms?
Yes. They both have all the characteristics required of a parallelogram. They both have opposite sides which are equal in length and parallel, they have opposite angles which are equal and their diagonals bisect each other.

There is one further quadrilateral which is also a special case of parallelogram and that is the **rhombus**. A rhombus has four sides that are equal in length. Opposite sides are parallel and opposite angles are of equal size. The diagonals bisect each other at right angles. A rhombus has at least 2 lines of reflective symmetry and rotational symmetry of order 2. If the interior angles of the rhombus are equal (i.e. 90°) then it is a square.

Another quadrilateral that has characteristics which can be satIsfied by many of the other quadrilaterals above is the **trapezium**. Generally a trapezium has one pair of parallel sides. As can be seen from the diagram on page 82, it does not need to have any other characteristics regarding symmetry properties, length of sides, size of angles or diagonals to be a trapezium. However, if a trapezium has 'legs' of equal length it is a special case of trapezium.

An **isosceles trapezium** has one pair of parallel sides, the other pair of sides is equal in length (remember 'same legs'?). It also has base angles which are the same size and diagonals which are equal in length. It has a line of reflective symmetry.

Looking at the definition of a trapezium it is clear that a square, a rectangle, a parallelogram and a rhombus could all be considered as a trapezium.

The final quadrilateral is the **kite**. This has two adjacent pairs of sides that are equal in length and at least one pair of opposite angles equal. The diagonals cross at right angles. A kite has at least one line of reflective symmetry. A rhombus and a square can also be considered a kite.

Congruence, similarity and 2-D transformations

Think about this

In a geoboard investigation the children are asked to find as many different triangles as possible. Kylie finds 12.

What does this tell you about Kylie's understanding of congruence, similarity and 2-D transformations?

Kylie does not yet understand the concept of congruence. What knowledge do you need to support your teaching of her?

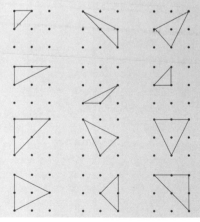

CONGRUENCE

Shapes are said to be congruent if they are the same shape and size. The orientation and position of the shapes do not matter as they do not alter the shape itself.

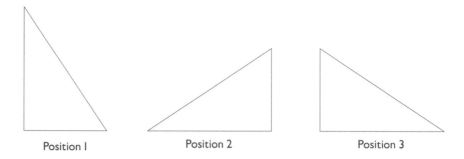

Position 1   Position 2   Position 3

Are these triangles congruent? What transformations have taken place?

These triangles are congruent as they are the same shape and size. The orientation and position have altered but the shape and size remain unchanged. In order to move from position 1 to position 2 the triangle was first **rotated** then **translated.** In order to move from position 2 to position 3 the triangle was **reflected**. Here it is necessary to further consider the **2-D transformations** which have taken place.

2-D TRANSFORMATIONS

There are a range of 2-D transformations which can be applied to shapes, including translation, reflection, rotation and enlargement.

For more information on transformation, see page 93 for the section on co-ordinates in four quadrants.

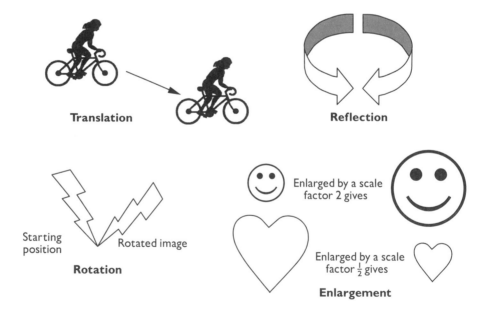

2-D transformations

- **A** *translation* **takes place when a shape is moved from one place to another just by sliding it (without rotating, reflecting or enlarging). The cyclist (above) has been translated. She has not changed size (enlargement) or orientation (reflection or rotation), she has solely changed position; therefore the two images are congruent.**

- When a shape is *reflected* a mirror image is created. The shape and size remain unchanged. Here again the two images are congruent. The position and orientation have changed due to the reflection, but the shape and size remain the same.
- *Rotation* involves a turn around a fixed point. In the above diagram the lightning bolt has been rotated 90° clockwise about the 'point'. Again the two images are congruent. The rotation has caused the orientation to change but not the size or shape.
- In mathematics *enlargement* can also mean getting smaller! Enlargement is also sometimes called scaling, as in order to change the size it is necessary to decide on a *scale factor* and a centre of enlargement. The scale factor is the number by which you multiply each measurement to achieve the enlargement. If the number is a fraction then the size is reduced. Enlargement is a 2-D transformation which does not result in two congruent images. Often the orientation remains unchanged; however, the size differs.

SIMILARITY

Shapes are said to be similar if all the angles are the same size and the shapes are the same but of a different size, i.e. one is an enlargement of the other.

These two triangles are similar because all their interior angles are the same size. For any triangles, if their interior angles are the same size they must be similar.

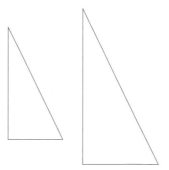

Kylie has no understanding of the concept of congruence. In order to develop this concept she will need to study 2-D transformations to establish whether shape, size, position and orientation have been maintained, i.e. to establish whether the resulting shape is congruent or similar.

Area of 2-D shapes

Think about this

Zak is asked to calculate the area of the following shape:

3 cm

4 cm

The answer is calculated as 14 cm.

What does this tell you about his understanding of calculating the area of a rectangle?

Firstly it is clear that Zak has recorded the answer as a linear measurement, i.e. in a straight line, hence the answer is expressed in cm. He has not attempted to calculate a 2-D measurement of area. In fact the answer calculated is that of the perimeter (length around the outside) of the shape.

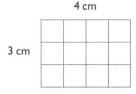

4 cm

RECTANGLE

In order to calculate the area of this rectangle a range of different methods could be used. The simplest would probably be counting squares.

3 cm

From this it can be seen that the area is 12 cm².

An extension of this method would be to multiply the base by the height. Why does this work?

In the diagram above it can be seen that in order to count squares accurately it is necessary to be systematic. Start in the top left-hand square and count across the top row, 1, 2, 3, 4. Next, move to the second row and repeat, 5, 6, 7, 8. Finally the bottom row, 9, 10, 11, 12. It can be seen from this that the rectangle has an area of three lots of four squares or 3 × 4 cm².

How does this help when calculating the areas of other plane shapes?

TRIANGLE

In a right-angled triangle it is quite straightforward to see that the area must be equal to $\frac{1}{2}$ × base × height:

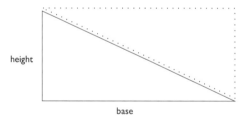

height

base

If a second, congruent triangle is positioned next to the right-angled triangle in question, it forms a rectangle. It has already been shown above that the area of a rectangle is equal to base × height; this triangle must therefore have an area equal to one half the area of the rectangle.

Is this true for all triangles?

Let's take an example of a triangle without a right angle.

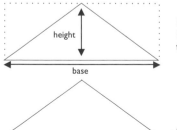

height

base

It is clear from this that the triangle can still be placed within a rectangle, but is the triangle still half the area of the rectangle?

By rearranging the triangles above, it can clearly be seen that the two large triangles each have the same area, i.e. half that of the rectangle. This is true for all triangles.

But what about parallelograms?

PARALLELOGRAM

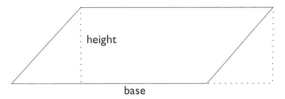

By cutting the parallelogram along the dotted line and repositioning the triangle at the opposite end of the parallelogram, a rectangle is achieved. The height and base measurements of this rectangle are exactly the same as those of the original parallelogram; to calculate the area of a parallelogram is therefore as straightforward as calculating the area of a rectangle, i.e. base × height.

How does this relate to the trapezium?

TRAPEZIUM

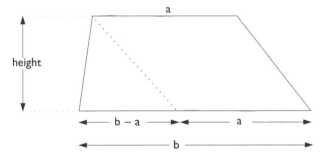

When calculating the area of a trapezium it is necessary to divide it into simpler shapes first. From the diagram above, it can be seen that a trapezium easily divides into a parallelogram and a triangle. Previous sections have already dealt with calculating these areas. The length of the base has been divided into two to enable the calculation to take place.

- **The area of the parallelogram is equal to a × h.**
- **The area of the triangle is equal to $\frac{1}{2}$ × (b – a) × h.**
- **To calculate the area of the trapezium it is necessary to add these two measurements:**

$$\begin{aligned}
\text{Area of the trapezium} &= ah + \tfrac{1}{2}(b-a)h \\
&= ah + \tfrac{1}{2}bh - \tfrac{1}{2}ah \\
&= \tfrac{1}{2}(a+b)h
\end{aligned}$$

Circle

A circle is a different kind of plane shape. It is not a polygon, i.e. it does not have straight sides. (Remember 'polygon'? A circle has no knees!)

For more information on irrational numbers, see page 33 for the section on rational and irrational numbers.

Calculating areas and circumferences of circles involves the use of the irrational number π. As π is irrational it means the number of decimal places is infinite. The fact that we use an estimation for π in calculations implies that any measure of area or circumference is only an **approximation**!

WHAT IS π ?

π (**Pi**) is found when the circumference of a circle is divided by the diameter:

$$\pi = \frac{\text{circumference}}{\text{diameter}}$$

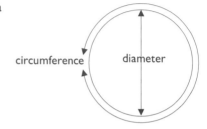

It is approximately equal to 3.141592...

If you use string to measure around a circle and to measure the diameter, and then divide one result by the other, you will obtain an answer as close to 3.14 as the accuracy of the method allows. This will be true for a circle of any size. As the diameter increases, the circumference increases but always maintaining the ratio.

The value of π has been calculated with ever increasing accuracy. The ancient Egyptian 'Rhind Papyrus' has the earliest recording of a value for π of $\frac{256}{81}$, which is about 3.16049. Archimedes (287–212 BCE) calculated π as 3.1419, which is close to today's value. In 1989 the Chudnovsky brothers found π to a billion digits! In 1997 Kanada and Takahasi calculated it to $51\frac{1}{2}$ billion digits!

USING π TO CALCULATE THE CIRCUMFERENCE OF A CIRCLE

Because the value of π is obtained by dividing the circumference (C) by the diameter (d), it can be seen that to find the circumference, π is simply multiplied by the diameter:

If $\pi = \frac{C}{d}$ then C = πd or C = 2πr (where r is equal to the radius).

USING π TO CALCULATE THE AREA OF A CIRCLE

It is possible to show this in a number of ways but the one which probably best models it is shown below. Firstly you have to imagine the circle cut into lots of **sectors**. Next you have to rearrange them as shown. Now imagine the sectors becoming smaller and smaller. As this happens the shape they are forming when rearranged becomes closer and closer to a rectangle. But what are the dimensions of the rectangle? It is quite easy to see that the width of the rectangle is equal to the radius of the circle. The length is also quite straightforward. As half of the sectors are placed facing one direction and the other half are facing the opposite direction, to make the opposite sides of the rectangle, it can be seen that the length is equal to half of the circumference.

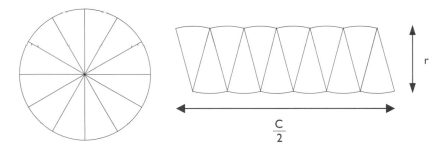

How does this help us calculate the area of the circle?

In order to calculate the area of the circle we simply need to calculate the area of the corresponding rectangle of which we know the dimensions.

$$\text{Area of the rectangle} = \text{length} \times \text{breadth}$$
$$= \frac{C}{2} \times r$$

We already know that $C = 2\pi r$, so substituting gives:

$$\text{Area} = \frac{2\pi r}{2} \times r$$
$$= \pi r \times r$$
$$= \pi r^2$$

Once we can calculate the circumference and area of a circle, sectors and arcs are very straightforward.

SECTORS AND ARCS

To find the arc of this circle we use the fact that we know the angle is $30°$ and that there are $360°$ in the full circle. This gives the arc as a fraction of the whole circumference, i.e. $\frac{30}{360}$. If the circumference is multiplied by this fraction the answer is equal to the length of the arc.

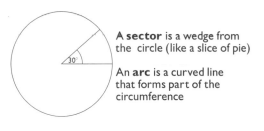

A **sector** is a wedge from the circle (like a slice of pie)

An **arc** is a curved line that forms part of the circumference

$$\text{Length of the arc} = \frac{30}{360} \times 2\pi r$$

$$= \frac{\pi r}{6}$$

The same method is applied to calculating the area of a sector. We know the sector in this case is $\frac{30}{360}$ of the total area of the circle. To find the sector's area the total area is simply multiplied by the fraction that is the sector. In this case:

$$\text{Area of the sector} = \frac{30}{360} \times \pi r^2$$

3-D shape

Think about this

Beth was asked to identify the number of faces, edges and vertices in the following solids:

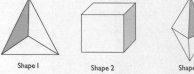

Shape 1   Shape 2   Shape 3

She gave the following answers:

	Faces	Edges	Vertices
Shape 1	4	4	6
Shape 2	6	8	12
Shape 3	8	6	12

What does this tell you about her understanding of defining 3-D shapes?

It is clear that Beth does not fully understand the terms 'face', 'edge' and 'vertex'. What subject knowledge will you need to be able to support her within class?

So far, this chapter has focused on 2-D shape. However, we live in a 3-D world and therefore need to recognise properties and characteristics of 3-D shapes in order to gain a fuller understanding of spatial concepts.

The shapes shown to Beth are all polyhedra. 'Polyhedron' comes from '*poly*' meaning 'many' and '*hedron*' from the Indo-European word meaning 'seat'. Hence polyhedron means 'many seats'. A polyhedron is a solid formed from flat faces. But what are faces, edges and vertices?

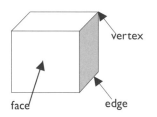

Face – the flat surfaces of solid shapes (i.e. parts of planes).

Edge – the line where two faces join (i.e. the intersection of two plane faces of a solid).

Vertex – the point of intersection of edges.

As with polygons there are some regular polyhedra. Incredibly there are only five regular polyhedra. A polyhedron is defined as regular if all its faces are congruent and all the angles between the faces (i.e. the dihedral angles) are the same size. This means that the shape will look the same regardless of which face it is 'sitting' on.

THE PLATONIC SOLIDS
The five regular polyhedra form a group of solids known as the **Platonic solids**. The five solids are the **regular tetrahedron**, the **cube**, the **regular octahedron**, the

regular dodecahedron and the **regular icosahedron**. The Platonic solids have been known since the time of the ancient Greeks. They were described by Plato in 350 BCE and hence now bear his name. The fact that there can only be five was proved by Euclid (325–270 BCE).

There is an interesting relationship between the number of faces, edges and vertices of the Platonic solids:

Solid	Faces	Edges	Vertices
Tetrahedron	4	6	4
Cube	6	12	8
Octahedron	8	12	6
Dodecahedron	12	30	20
Icosahedron	20	30	12

From this table the relationship between the number of faces, edges and vertices can be seen:

$$\text{Faces} + \text{Vertices} = \text{Edges} + 2 \qquad \text{or} \qquad F + V = E + 2$$

This is called **Euler's formula** and applies not only to the Platonic solids (i.e. regular solids) but also to a great many other solids, almost certainly all those that will be encountered within a primary school. Euler's formula is named after Leonard Euler who proved this formula in 1735.

Polyhedra are named as consistently as polygons, not only the regular polyhedra but also the irregular ones. In the diagram of **pyramids** on the right, one of the shapes is a pentahedron and the other is a heptahedron.

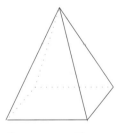 

Square pyramid   Hexagonal pyramid

Other polyhedra can be classified together to form particular groups.

PYRAMIDS
Pyramids are solids that have a polygon base and triangular faces. It is easy to decide what to call each pyramid as it takes its name from the shape of its base; for example, a square pyramid or a hexagonal pyramid.

PRISMS

Prisms are a different group of solids. They each have a uniform cross-section. This means that if you cut them anywhere along their length, parallel to their base, you will always obtain a shape that is identical to the base shape.

Rectangular prism   Triangular prism

As with pyramids, prisms take their names from the shape of their base, hence the rectangular and triangular prisms above.

NETS

A net is a flat shape that can be folded to form a solid. Any polyhedron has a number of different nets. For example, the cube has 11 possible nets. Three possible cube nets are shown below:

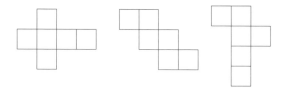

Nets for some irregular polyhedra are shown below. For which of the solids are they the nets?

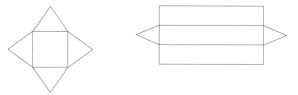

The first is the net of a square pyramid (or pentahedron); the second is the net of a triangular prism (also a pentahedron).

SURFACE AREA AND VOLUME

 For more information on how to calculate surface areas of polyhedra, see page 68 for the section on surface area.

The surface area of a polyhedron is equal to the sum of the areas of its faces and is measured in square units, e.g. cm^2. The volume of a solid is the amount of space it takes up. It is measured in cubic units, e.g. cm^3.

For Beth, developing a greater understanding of the correct mathematical vocabulary of 3-D shapes will ensure accuracy as further spatial concepts are introduced.

This chapter has concentrated on shapes and transformations, but it is also very important to be able to express where in space something is located. This requires a consideration of **Cartesian co-ordinates**.

Cartesian co-ordinates

Think about this

Sam was asked to plot the following pairs of Cartesian co-ordinates:

(2,1) (2,3) (6,1) (6,3)

He produced the following result:

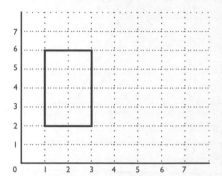

What does this tell you about Sam's understanding of Cartesian co-ordinates in the first quadrant?

Sam does not understand that the first number represents the distance travelled along the x-axis and the second number represents the distance travelled along the y-axis. What subject knowledge do you need to effectively support your teaching of Sam?

Cartesian co-ordinates are named after the French philosopher and scientist René Descartes (1596–1650). It is vital that co-ordinates are read correctly, otherwise they are completely inaccurate. The first number (the **abscissa**) always represents the distance along the x-axis (horizontal axis), and the second number (the **ordinate**) the distance travelled along the y-axis (vertical axis). There are plenty of ways of remembering this, e.g. 'bottoms up!', 'along the corridor then up the stairs', OUT – 'Out and Up To it'.

Sam was working with co-ordinates in the first quadrant only. However, it is important to know that we can work with co-ordinates in four quadrants, and indeed three dimensions. This book will not consider 3-D co-ordinates, but if you are interested there are lots of websites containing a wealth of information.

CO-ORDINATES IN FOUR QUADRANTS
Just as in the first quadrant, the first number represents the distance along the x-axis and the second number the distance along the y-axis. The only difference in four quadrants is that the numbers may be negative. Look at the following diagram and try to decide the co-ordinates before reading on.

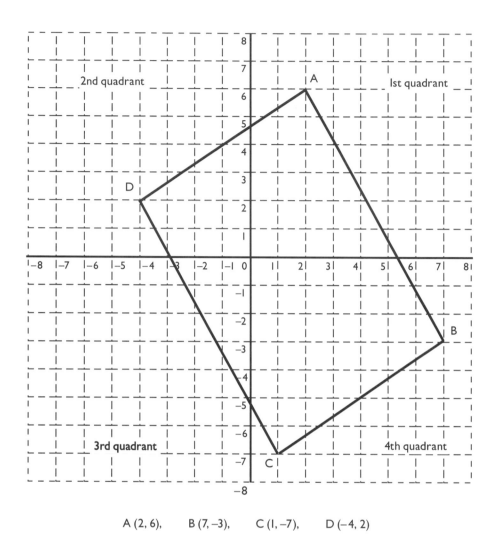

A (2, 6),   B (7, –3),   C (1, –7),   D (–4, 2)

Co-ordinates in four quadrants

2-D transformations can also be represented in this way. It is possible to identify relationships between the sets of co-ordinates of the original shape and its image after transformation (see page 95).

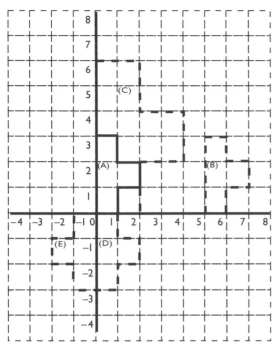

Shape (A) has co-ordinates (0,0), (1,0), (1,1), (2,1), (2,2), (1,2), (1,3), (0,3)
It has been transformed in a number of different ways. To move to position (B) it has been **translated**.

The co-ordinates for image (B) are: (5,0) (6,0), (6,1), (7,1), (7,2), (6,2), (6,3), (5,3)

Because the shape has been translated along the x-axis, it is only the x values which change. If it had translated along the y-axis the y values would change.

2-D transformations represented by co-ordinates in four quadrants

To create image (C) shape (A) has been **enlarged**. The new co-ordinates are:

(0,0) (2,0) (2,2) (4,2) (4,4) (2,4) (2,6) (0,6)

Because shape (A) has been enlarged by a scale factor 2, each co-ordinate has been multiplied by 2.

To create image (D) shape (A) has been reflected in the x-axis. The new co-ordinates are:

(0,0) (1,0) (1,−1) (2,−1) (2,−2) (1,−2) (1,−3) (0,−3)

The result is that the y value for each of the co-ordinates is now negative, i.e. it has been multiplied by −1. Reflection in the y-axis would result in the x value being multiplied by −1.

To create image (E) shape (A) has been rotated 180° clockwise about the origin (0,0). The new co-ordinates are:

(0,0) (−1,0) (−1,−1) (−2,−1) (−2,−2) (−1,−2) (−1,−3) (0,−3)

The result here is that both x and y values have been multiplied by −1. This is because the new image is in the 3rd quadrant. If (A) was rotated 90° clockwise about the origin, the x and y values would swap and the new y value would be multiplied by −1. This happens because the orientation changes and the image is in the 4th quadrant. A 270° clockwise rotation about the origin again results in the x and y values swapping, owing to the new orientation, but this time the new x value is multiplied by -1 because the image is in the 2nd quadrant.

For Sam, the first thing to learn is the meaning of the co-ordinates in order to support wider study within this area.

Shape and Space:

a summary of key points

—— *Polygons are plane shapes with many angles.*

—— *Polygons are named systematically.*

—— *A regular polygon has all sides of equal length and all interior angles of equal size.*

—— *A shape is said to have reflective symmetry if you can fold it so that one half fits exactly on top of the other half.*

—— *A shape is said to have rotational symmetry if it looks the same in different positions when rotated about its centre.*

—— *2-D transformations include translation, reflection, rotation and enlargement.*

—— *Shapes are congruent if they are the same shape and size, regardless of orientation and position.*

—— *Shapes are similar if all the angles are the same size and the shapes are the same but of a different size, i.e. one is an enlargement of the other.*

—— *Polyhedra are solid shapes with many faces.*

—— *Polyhedra are named systematically.*

—— *A polyhedron is defined as regular if all its faces are congruent and all the angles between the faces (i.e. the dihedral angles) are the same size.*

—— *Cartesian co-ordinates can be used to express where something is located in space.*

✔ Self-assessment questions

1 How many different quadrilaterals can you name which have at least the following characteristics:

- opposite sides equal in length and parallel;
- opposite angles equal;
- diagonals bisect each other?

2 Find the area of the following triangle:

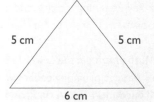

5 cm   5 cm   **(Hint: Pythagoras might help!)**

6 cm

3 A new hopscotch game is to be painted on a playground. On the plan the game is 2 cm wide and 7 cm long. The game on the playground will be similar to the one on the plan. If the playground game is to be 60 cm wide, how long will it be?

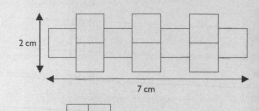

2 cm

7 cm

4 Add two squares to each of these shapes to make them have exactly 2 lines of symmetry.

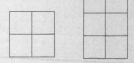

5 Add two squares to each of the following shapes to make them have rotational symmetry of order 4.

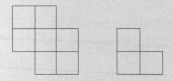

6 (a) Hexominoes are formed when 6 identical squares are joined contiguously, i.e. they are touching along at least one side, not just corner to corner. How many different, i.e not congruent, hexominoes are there? (Clue: there are more than 11 as we already know that 11 of them form nets for the cube. Can you identify the 11 cube nets as a subset of the hexominoes?)

(b) Applying consistent naming for polyhedra, what would be an alternative name for the cube?

Further reading

Cockburn, A. (1999) *Teaching Mathematics with Insight: the Identification, Diagnosis and Remediation of Young Children's Mathematical Errors*. London: Falmer Press. This book clearly identifies intrinsic problems with mathematics of both a psychological and mathematical nature. It aims to increase understanding of primary mathematics and thus to develop primary practice. It focuses on four areas – place value, subtraction, time and shape.

Haylock, D. (2001) *Mathematics Explained for Primary Teachers*. London: Paul Chapman Publishing. As the title suggests, this book explains much of the content of the primary mathematics curriculum. It also addresses key teaching points and gives opportunities to try some self-assessment questions in each area, to further support your subject knowledge development.

Haylock, D. and Cockburn, A. (1997) *Understanding Mathematics in the Lower Primary Years*. London: Paul Chapman Publishing. This book aims to provide readers with a clearer understanding of the mathematics they will encounter in the classroom. Its focuses include mathematical symbolism and developing appropriate mathematical language. It is written for those involved with the teaching of 4- to 8-year-olds.

Williams, E. and Shuard, H. (1997) *Primary Mathematics Today*. Harlow: Longman. This book is an extremely comprehensive text covering all aspects of primary mathematics. It supports subject knowledge development very effectively while at the same time considering pedagogical issues and clearly detailing progression.

Introduction

Statistics are used to help us make sense of the world around us. We are surrounded by a lot of data and by using statistics we can bring order to this data and draw information from it. Teachers deal with statistics often when marking work, target setting, dealing with National Curriculum test results and presenting information for external agencies. This chapter has intentionally used examples that are not specifically related to the data you may come across when teaching. This is because the examples chosen have been designed for you to have a more grounded understanding of the use of statistics in common everyday experiences, just like the data your pupils will be exploring in mathematics.

Probability came about as we began to make sense of the world around us. We use it to predict the future once we have made some sense of the past. We use probability often in our everyday lives. We forecast the weather according to the probability of rain, and this is based on our knowledge about weather patterns, etc. Many people try to 'beat the odds' when trying to win money in the lottery, football pools and the races.

Professional Standards for QTS

 ### 2.1b

To achieve QTS you need to have a secure knowledge and understanding of the mathematics content of the National Curriculum for Key Stages 1 and 2 and the methods and expectations set out in the National Numeracy Strategy. For statistics and probability this includes:

- *using discrete and continuous data and understanding the difference between them;*
- *tabulating and representing data diagrammatically and graphically;*
- *interpreting data and predicting from data;*
- *finding and using the mean and other central measures;*
- *finding and using measures of spread to compare distributions;*
- *using systematic methods for identifying, counting and organising events and outcomes;*
- *understanding the difference between probability and observed relative frequencies;*
- *recognise independent and mutually exclusive events.*

You may find it helpful to read through the appropriate section of the Handbook that accompanies the Standards for the award of QTS for clarification and support.

Curriculum Guidance for the Foundation Stage, the National Curriculum and the National Numeracy Strategy

The Curriculum Guidance for the Foundation Stage section on mathematical development highlights the need for pupils to use language such as 'more' or 'less', 'greater' or 'smaller', 'heavier' or 'lighter', to compare two numbers or quantities (QCA, 1999). This encourages an early introduction to handling data generally as well as leading into the areas of statistics and probability.

Within the Mathematics National Curriculum for England, the Programmes of Study set out the knowledge, skills and understanding which are to be taught throughout the Key Stages. These are closely linked to the Key Objectives identified for each year group within the NNS *Framework for Teaching Mathematics*. Knowledge of probability and statistics is helpful in teaching number and handling data. Within the Key Stage 1 Programme of Study, Number, processing, representing and handling data involves simple statistics work using lists, tables and charts to sort, classify and organise information. By Key Stage 2, pupils are expected to use and apply their data-handling skills in order to process, represent and interpret data. Early probability concepts join statistics at this level.

Knowledge and understanding

Statistics: collecting data

DISCRETE AND CONTINUOUS DATA

We can collect data in two ways: by counting or by measuring. When we can count the data, we call them **discrete data**. That is, there is a discrete category which the item that we have counted can fall into and it is possible to list these. An example of this is favourite pastimes. We can say that 23 people prefer angling and 18 people prefer bungee jumping, but these two pastimes are not connected in any way. In fact it would be very difficult to fish while jumping off a bridge!

Continuous data, however, are measured. These data do not fit into specific discrete categories because the data can be placed anywhere along a line of measurement. It is not possible to list all the outcomes. Imagine, for example, the height of a growing child. At any stage during their life a measurement can be taken. This measurement is continuous. There was a continual growth between the two measurements taken of the child's height at 93 cm and at 106 cm. An infinite number of heights could have been measured between the time these two heights were recorded.

Another example is a horse steeplechase race. It would be possible to measure the speed at which the horses are travelling at any point during the race. The speed that a horse is travelling around the course and over jumps will change according to whether it is jumping or galloping, the part of the race that is being run or indeed where the horse is placed within the pack.

It is important to understand the difference between discrete and continuous data because the type of data must be known before organising the collection of data. Discrete and continuous data are represented graphically in different ways also. This will be discussed in the next section.

Methods of recording and representing data

It is possible to collect and record data using a variety of methods. Before deciding on a method of recording data, it is imperative that you know the *type* of data that you are collecting and what you want to find out. Being clear in your mind about what you are collecting and why you are collecting it will mean that you collect only the data you require in a way that is useful for you to record, represent and interpret.

It is possible to gather data by asking questions and recording the responses on questionnaires or in tables. It is also possible to collect data by measuring and recording these data in tabular form. Sometimes it is possible to find the data already recorded in other places such as books, CD-ROMs, the Internet or other databases. It is possible to create paper- or electronic-based methods of recording data such as databases and spreadsheets.

This section outlines the various methods of recording data and representing it in tabular and graphical forms.

TABLES

Tables are a useful method for both collecting and representing data. Data are easy to compile and read from a table. Let's use the example of favourite pastimes again. The figure below shows two tables of favourite pastimes. In Table 1, the data were collected using tally marks. Table 2 has the tally marks counted up.

FAVOURITE PASTIME	NUMBER OF PEOPLE
Angling	||| ||| ||| ||| ||| |||
Bungee Jumping	||| ||| ||| |||
Cycling	||| ||| ||| ||| ||| ||| ||
Fencing	||| ||| ||| ||
Reading	|||
Rock Climbing	||| ||| |||
Playing Cards	
Walking	||| ||| ||

Table 1

FAVOURITE PASTIME	NUMBER OF PEOPLE
Angling	23
Bungee Jumping	18
Cycling	27
Fencing	17
Reading	3
Rock Climbing	15
Playing Cards	0
Walking	12

Table 2

Recording data in tables

From Table 2 it is easy to read how many people state angling to be their favourite pastime. Table 1 is, in some ways, easier to gather information from. We can see at a glance which pastime is the most popular because there are more tally marks. It is important to consider the presentation of data in terms of what information needs to be gathered from it.

GRAPHS AND DIAGRAMS

It is often easier to read data from graphs and diagrams rather than tables when wanting to begin to interpret data and predict from it. The following are the diagrams and graphs that you need to be familiar with. The earlier graphs are not shown here as this book is aimed at your own level of subject knowledge and it is assumed that you are familiar with them. If you are unsure, you can also find them in the companion mathematics book in this series, called *Primary Mathematics: Teaching Theory and Practice*.

BLOCK GRAPH

Block graphs are used to display discrete data. One block can represent one item, or a number of items. It is necessary to have a key to explain how many items each block represents.

PICTOGRAPH

Pictographs are used to display discrete data. One picture/symbol can represent one item or a number of items. Again, it is necessary to have a key to explain how many items each symbol represents. It is equally necessary to ensure that each of the pictures/symbols are of a similar size and that if they represent many items then it is clear how many items they represent when they are not whole.

BAR GRAPH

Bar graphs are used to display discrete data. The length of each bar represents the number of items (the **frequency**). Each bar is separate to show that the data is discrete. Bar graphs can be drawn vertically and horizontally.

BAR-LINE GRAPH

Bar-line graphs display the same information as bar graphs. Lines are used instead of bars to represent the frequency of the data.

PIE CHART

Pie charts are a circle graph cut into sectors. By calculating the fraction of the circle, the percentage of the circle, or the degrees of the circle it is possible to make each sector. Pie charts allow a graphical representation of the proportions of the data easily.

LINE GRAPH

Line graphs are used to display continuous data. A line graph of the speed of steeplechase horses will rise and fall according to the section of the race they are running. A line graph of a child's height, however, is probably going to increase, as is a graph showing the distance travelled in a car on a journey.

SCATTERGRAPH

Scattergraphs are used to compare two sets of data. These data can be discrete or continuous. The example on the right compares the height of Year 5 children with the length of their waist.

It is possible to make decisions about the correlation between the two sets of data, and lines of best fit. When comparing the data, scattergraphs allow us to draw conclusions about correlations between the two sets of data.

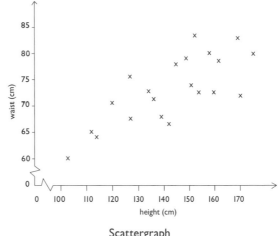

Scattergraph

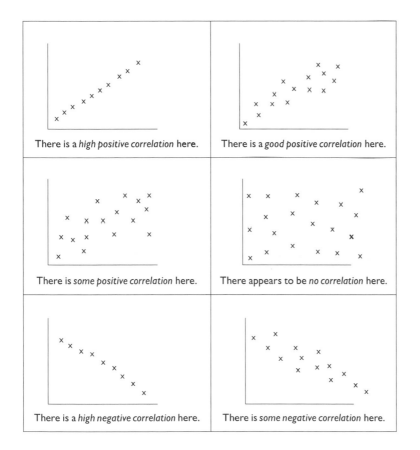

There is a *high positive correlation* here.

There is a *good positive correlation* here.

There is *some positive correlation* here.

There appears to be *no correlation* here.

There is a *high negative correlation* here.

There is *some negative correlation* here.

Correlation

FREQUENCY DIAGRAM

Frequency diagrams are used with continuous data. The data are grouped into classes. On the right, there is a frequency diagram of the weight of a class of children in Year 6. In this example there are eight children who weigh less than 50kg and more than, or equal to, 45kg.

Weight (kg)	Frequency
30 ≤ W < 35	2
35 ≤ W < 40	5
40 ≤ W < 45	10
45 ≤ W < 50	8
50 ≤ W < 55	6
55 ≤ W < 60	3
60 ≤ W < 65	1

Frequency diagram

Histogram showing the weight
of Year 5 pupils

FREQUENCY HISTOGRAM

Histograms graphically represent continuous data. Unlike a bar graph, the 'bars' of the histogram touch. In each 'bar', the *area* represents the frequency. In this example, the class intervals are the same width, so the heights of the 'bars' are in proportion with their frequencies. Sometimes this is not the case, and you will need to look at the areas of the histogram more carefully.

CUMULATIVE FREQUENCY

Sometimes it is necessary to use a **cumulative** frequency. The cumulative frequency diagram here has used the data from above. From this diagram it is easy to read how many pupils weigh less than, say, 55 kg.

Upper bound	Cumulative frequency
< 35	2
< 40	7
< 45	17
< 50	25
< 55	31
< 60	34
< 65	35

Cumulative frequency diagram

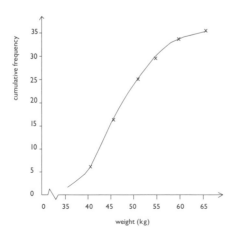

CUMULATIVE FREQUENCY CURVE

It is possible to graph the cumulative frequency data from above in a **curve**. The points of the cumulative data are plotted and then usually joined together with curves (although sometimes line segments are also used).

Cumulative frequency curve for the weight of Year 5 pupils

Interpreting data and predicting from data

Having collected and represented data, it is an equally important skill to be able to interpret the data and predict from it.

If the data were gathered with a specific question in mind, then the main part of the interpretation of the data will be to answer the question originally set. This is certainly a means to an end, where the data collection has been undertaken purely to answer a set question. Often, however, the interpretation of and prediction from data is not that straightforward. We are bombarded with data from many sources every day when watching the news on the television, listening to the news on the radio, or reading newspapers and magazines.

You have probably heard the old adage: 'lies, damn lies and statistics'. Statistics can be used to prove almost anything, if the statistician is clever (or naughty) enough! A graph once 'proved' that babies were indeed brought by storks, because a scattergraph that had been created showed a high positive correlation between nesting storks and the birthrate in a town suburb! It is therefore necessary, at times, to be sceptical about the data and graphical representations that you are presented with rather than accepting them at face value.

It may be necessary to ask questions about how the data were collected in order to ascertain possible sources of error and the limitations of the data collection. How accurate were the measurements? Were the questions asked openly, or could they have been asked in a misleading way making the data less accurate? How many people were asked? Did they all respond, or did only the people with the strongest views bother to reply?

It is important to question other aspects of the data. Often the representation of the data, once collected, can be equally misleading.

Data prediction

Sometimes data can be a powerful resource for predicting likely outcomes based on previous experience. It is possible to identify long-term and short-term features in time-series data. For example, if data were gathered about a steeplechase horse over a number of races, its trainer would be able to begin to build a profile about the horse's strengths and weaknesses. This information could be used to improve the training and the racing of the horse.

It is also possible to make and justify statements about relationships between variables in a sample as the result of a statistical investigation; for example, using scattergraphs.

From these populations, it is possible to make statistically based inferences about whole populations, and even confidently express reasoned opinions from the media.

Finding and using the mean and other central measures

The **mean**, or **arithmetic mean** (which is its correct name), is the most common type of **average** that is used. It is used in many everyday situations such as monthly temperature, runs per over in cricket and student marks. It is found by adding up all the components in a set of data and dividing the sum by the number of components in the set.

For example, the mean temperature in a country in the Southern Hemisphere in February is 19°C. The days within February vary quite a lot. Look at this list of temperatures:

20, 21, 19, 17, 16, 18, 17, 20, 19, 18, 21, 21, 18, 19, 18, 20, 21, 22, 20, 19, 19, 15, 16, 18, 20, 22, 21, 20

To find the mean temperature, the temperatures are added together, and then divided by the number of days in the month.

The sum of the temperatures is 535. When divided by the number of days in the month (28), the mean temperature is 19.1.

It is also possible to calculate the mean from a frequency distribution (see below). This is an easier method of finding the mean if there is a large amount of data.

Temperature (°C)	Frequency	Temp. × Frequency
x	f	fx
15	1	15
16	2	32
17	2	34
18	5	90
19	5	95
20	6	120
21	5	105
22	2	44
	28	535

Mean temperature $= \dfrac{\Sigma fx}{\Sigma f}$

$= \dfrac{\text{total of (temperature} \times \text{frequency)}}{\text{total number of days in the month}}$

Σ is **sigma**. It means 'the sum of'.

Calculating the mean from a frequency distribution

The **median** is the middle value in a set of data. In order to find the median, the data must first be put in order:

15, 16, 16, 17, 17, 18, 18, 18, 18, 18, 19, 19, 19, 19, 19, 20, 20, 20, 20, 20, 20, 21, 21, 21, 21, 21, 22, 22

Then it is necessary to find the middle value. You can do this by dividing the number of components in the set by two, or by counting in from the end values until you meet in the middle. In this example, there are 28 values. Because twenty-eight is an even number, it is possible to divide the set of data into two evenly. Therefore the middle is between two values. It happens that both of the values it lies between are 19, so the median is 19. Had it fallen between two values that were not the same, then the mean of those two numbers would be taken as the median. Had the set comprised the number of days in February in a leap year, the number of values present would have been 29. The median would have been the 15th value.

The position of the median $= \dfrac{(n + 1)}{2}$

$$= \dfrac{28 + 1}{2}$$

$$= 14.5$$

The **mode** is the value that occurs most commonly in any set of data. In the temperature example, the temperature that occurs most commonly is 20°C. There were six days that reached 20 degrees, so the mode for this set of data is 20. Other frequent temperatures are 18, 19 and 21. Each of these occurred five times. Had 20°C also occurred five times in February (instead of six), then there would have been four modes for this set of data!

Why are the mean, median and mode sometimes different from each other? In our example, the mean and median of the February temperatures are 19°C. The mode, however, is 20°C. If you look at the data carefully, you will note that there was one cooler day where the temperature was recorded at only 15°C. This unusually cool temperature for the month has meant that the extreme value has had an impact on calculating the mean.

WHEN ARE THE MEAN, MEDIAN AND MODE BEST USED?
The mean is the most common measure of average. It is used to compare different sets of data. For example, now that we have the mean temperature of February in one country, we could compare it with other countries' mean temperatures or even other months of the same country to look at the climate, perhaps with a view to going on holiday.

It is useful to look at the median when working with small sets of data. The median is not affected by extreme values within the data, such as the 15°C in the temperature example.

Sometimes, it is not appropriate to calculate the mean or the median. For example, if a group of people were planning a trip to the country discussed above, then it would be sensible to look at the most common temperatures, or the modal temperatures. The mode of the temperatures above is 20°C. So, it would make sense to pack mostly clothes that could be worn at 20°C, with fewer for 15°C.

Finding and using measures of spread to compare distributions

If we were planning a trip to the country where these temperatures were taken, we would want to look at the **range** of temperatures to ensure that we packed appropriate clothing for the holiday. It would be possible to compare the range of these temperatures with the range of temperatures from another country to look at the spread over the month of February. If we were looking for somewhere to pack a light bag, we might want to select a country that has a narrow spread of warm temperatures. The use of the range is the simplest method of finding and using a measure of spread to compare distributions.

BOX AND WHISKER DIAGRAMS

It is possible to use a **box and whisker diagram** to compare distributions graphically. This involves calculating the median as well as two other measures, called **quartiles**.

15, 16, 16, 17, 17, 18, 18, 18, 18, 18, 19, 19, 19, 19, 19, 20, 20, 20, 20, 20, 20, 21, 21, 21, 21, 21, 22, 22

Above are the temperatures of a country in the Southern Hemisphere in February. In the previous section we calculated the median by finding the middle temperature. We will use the same technique to find the quartiles. To find the **lower quartile**, it is necessary to ascertain one-quarter of the data. To find the **upper quartile**, it is necessary to ascertain three-quarters of the data.

There are 28 values in this example. Because twenty-eight is a multiple of 4, it is possible to divide the set of data into four evenly. Therefore each of the quartiles lies between two values:

15, 16, 16, 17, 17, 18, 18 | 18, 18, 18, 19, 19, 19, 19 | 19, 20, 20, 20, 20, 20, 20 | 21, 21, 21, 21, 21, 22, 22

If we look at the **lower quartile**, it happens that both values it lies between are 18, so the lower quartile is 18. The **upper quartile**, however, has fallen between two values that were not the same: 20 and 21. The mean of those two numbers is taken as the upper quartile, so the upper quartile is 20.5.

The position of the lower quartile $= \dfrac{(n + 1)}{4} = \dfrac{28 + 1}{4} = 7.25$

The position of the upper quartile $= \dfrac{3(n + 1)}{4} = \dfrac{3(28 + 1)}{4} = \dfrac{87}{4} = 21.75$

It is also possible to calculate the **interquartile range**. The **range** can be affected by extreme values, so using the interquartile range to compare sets of data removes the extreme values. The interquartile range is the range between the upper and lower quartiles.

Interquartile range = upper quartile − lower quartile
$$= 20.5 - 18$$
$$= 2.5$$

Having found the quartiles and the median, it is possible to graphically represent these data in a box and whisker diagram:

Box and whisker diagram

The interquartile range covers 50% of the data and each 'whisker' respresents 25% of the data. When two or more box and whisker diagrams are placed together, it is possible to make comparisons between them more easily than when looking at the raw data.

Probability: the probability scale

We use probability to describe how much we believe an **event** in the future is going to happen. In everyday discussion we use words such as 'certain' and 'unlikely' when we are talking about upcoming events. We can place these words on a **probability scale** like this:

In mathematics this probability scale becomes more formalised as fractions, percentages or decimals replace these words. For example, an event that is certain to happen has a probability of 1, or 100%, whereas an event that has an even chance of happening (such as tossing a coin to get a head) has a probability of $\frac{1}{2}$, 50% or 0.5:

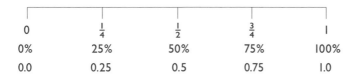

HOW CAN WE IDENTIFY THE PROBABILITY OF AN EVENT?

It is only possible to make an objective statement about the probability of an event if you have some prior knowledge about the event. For example, it would not be possible to make a statement about the probability of iguanas in South America mating this month unless you know about iguanas in South America, or you know something about the mating season of iguanas and you know about the weather in South America!

There are three ways that you can have some knowledge about an event:

- **The first is based on** *prior knowledge*: it may be possible to ascertain previous statistical data and work from this. This is used most often in the everyday world. This type of probability is used in calculating insurance premiums, choosing investments and forecasting the weather.
- **The second is to undertake an experiment to re-enact the event.** This often occurs in the fields of science and mathematics where many experiments take place to ensure the safety of a chemical, introduced species, or vehicle air bags, etc. The more the experiment is undertaken, or in the long run, the closer to the expected outcome we should be. The *experimental probability* (also known as relative frequency) can be calculated by dividing the number of outcomes by the total number of trials.

$$\text{experimental probability} = \frac{\text{number of successful outcomes}}{\text{total number of trials}}$$

- **The third is to use the theoretical knowledge about the event to predict an outcome.** We know that there is an even chance of getting a 'tail' when we toss a coin, because there are two possible, even outcomes before tossing the coin: a head and a tail. The *theoretical probability* can be calculated by dividing the number of actual outcomes by the total number of possible outcomes.

$$\text{theoretical probability} = \frac{\text{number of successful outcomes}}{\text{total number of possible outcomes}}$$

If we toss one coin, we can get a head or a tail. The probability of getting a head is $\frac{1}{2}$. The probability of getting a tail is $\frac{1}{2}$ also.

$$\tfrac{1}{2} + \tfrac{1}{2} = 1.$$

Practical task

If we toss the coin once and get a head, what is the probability of throwing a head the next time?

The probability is $\frac{1}{2}$. The probability does not change depending on what has gone before. Every time we toss the coin, there is still an even chance of tossing a head or a tail. The events are **mutually exclusive**.

If we throw a die, the possible outcomes are 1, 2, 3, 4, 5 or 6. The probability of throwing any one of these numbers is $\frac{1}{6}$.

$$\tfrac{1}{6} + \tfrac{1}{6} + \tfrac{1}{6} + \tfrac{1}{6} + \tfrac{1}{6} + \tfrac{1}{6} = 1.$$

Just as with the coin tossing, any prior throws of the die do not have an impact on the probability of throwing a 1, 2, 3, 4, 5 or 6 in the next throw. Again, the events are mutually exclusive.

The probabilities of all the possible mutually exclusive events always add up to 1.

What is the difference between theoretical and experimental probability?

In the previous section we talked about three ways of making an informed judgement about the probability of an event happening. Two of these were theoretical and experimental probability.

Practical task

Toss a coin. Record in an efficient way whether you get a head or a tail. Keep doing this for about a minute. If there are a number of you working together, use your own coins and add the number of times you each tossed a head and a tail at the end to carry out a larger experiment.

Prior to starting, what did you expect your outcome to be? If you thought that the number of times you tossed a head would be the same as the number of times you tossed a tail, you were using theoretical probability that tells you the probability of throwing a tail or a head is even. You have now found that the experimental probability is not as accurate as you may originally have thought! You may toss three or four heads in a row, or even more, but every time you toss the coin, the probability of getting a head is still $\frac{1}{2}$. The more times you toss the coin (in other words, undertake the experiment), the closer you will get to the expected outcome.

Think about this

Tamine in your class complains that she does not like a game you have set them to play. To start, she needs to throw a six and she complains that throwing a six is harder than any other number.

What knowledge do you need to have in order to help Tamine to understand about the probability of throwing a six?

You will need to know that there are six possible outcomes when throwing a die. These outcomes are 1, 2, 3, 4, 5 or 6. You will also need to know that there is only one successful outcome when throwing a six, because the die only has one six on it. So, the theoretical probability of throwing a six, written as P(6), is $\frac{1}{6}$. This also means, there-fore, that Tamine has a probability of $\frac{5}{6}$ of *not* throwing a six! (This can be calculated by $1 - P(6)$, which is $1 - \frac{1}{6} = \frac{5}{6}$.) It is also important that you understand the difference between theoretical and experimental probability, because every time the die is thrown it is mutually exclusive of any other throw, meaning that at every single throw Tamine still has a probability of $\frac{1}{6}$ of getting a six.

When do I add two probabilities?

Let's keep working with a die. Imagine that you change the rules for Tamine in the above example. The rule is now that the child has to throw a 2 *or* a 6 to start. Does this make the game easier or harder to begin? Why?

Yes, it makes the game easier to begin because you can see that throwing a 2 or a 6 is more likely than throwing just a 6. Looking at this mathematically, in terms of probability, the probability of throwing a 6 is $\frac{1}{6}$. The probability of throwing a 2 is also $\frac{1}{6}$.

The probability of throwing a 2 or 6 on a die is:

$$P(2 \text{ or } 6) = P(2) + P(6) = \frac{1}{6} + \frac{1}{6} = \frac{2}{6} = \frac{1}{3}$$

When two mutually exclusive events (A and B) take place, the probability that *either* happens is:

$$P(A \text{ or } B) = P(A) + P(B)$$

Practical task

In a feely bag, place ten multilink of the following colours:

5 red   3 blue   2 yellow

- **Which colour are you most likely to draw out? Why?**
- **Which colour are you least likely to draw out? Why?**
- **Write down the probabilities of drawing out a red, blue or yellow multilink cube.**

The probability of drawing a red cube $= P(\text{Red})$ $= \frac{5}{10}$ $= \frac{1}{2}$

The probability of drawing a blue cube $= P(\text{Blue})$ $= \frac{3}{10}$

The probability of drawing a yellow cube $= P(\text{Yellow}) = \frac{2}{10}$ $= \frac{1}{5}$

$$\frac{5}{10} + \frac{3}{10} + \frac{2}{10} = \frac{10}{10} = 1$$

Again, the probabilities of all the possible mutually exclusive events add up to 1.

What is the probability that a red or a blue cube is drawn out?

$$P(\text{red or blue}) = P(\text{red}) + P(\text{blue}) = \frac{5}{10} + \frac{3}{10} = \frac{8}{10} = \frac{4}{5}$$

What is the probability that a cube that is drawn out is **not** red or blue?

$$P(\text{not red or blue}) = 1 - P(\text{red or blue}) = 1 - \frac{4}{5} = \frac{1}{5}$$

We can check that this is correct, because it is also the probability of drawing a yellow cube.

What about throwing two coins?

Think about this

You are undertaking a probability experiment in class with a group of Year 5 and 6 pupils where they are tossing two coins and looking at the outcomes. They have decided that there are three possible outcomes: they could toss two heads, a head and a tail, or two tails. They have decided that because there are three possible outcomes, the probability of tossing any of these combinations is $\frac{1}{3}$.

What knowledge will you need in order to help these pupils in their mathematics work?

In the examples above we have worked with mutually exclusive events. We will now explore what happens when we work with **two independent events**. It is often useful to use a systematic way to record the possible outcomes of two independent events. We will use coins again in this example, but we will be tossing two coins at a time.

When we toss two coins there are indeed three possible outcomes: two heads, a head and a tail, or two tails. The pupils' logic only falls down when they assume that each of these possible outcomes has **the same chance** of being thrown.

We can use a number of systematic methods to record what happens when two coins are tossed. We can list the outcomes, make a two-way table, or a tree diagram.

Simply listing the outcomes for this example is straightforward because there are only two outcomes for *each* of the coins. Coin 1 can give a head or a tail, and coin 2 can give a head or a tail. This listing shows the possible outcomes:

Coin 1	Coin 2
H	H
H	T
T	H
T	T

We could also use a two-way table to list the possible outcomes:

		Coin 2	
		Head (H)	Tail (T)
Coin 1	Head (H)	H H	H T
	Tail (T)	T H	T T

Finally, we could use a tree diagram to list the possible outcomes:

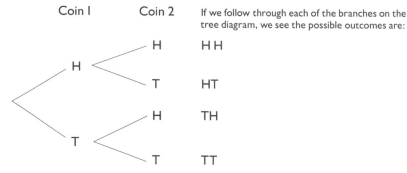

Coin I   Coin 2   If we follow through each of the branches on the tree diagram, we see the possible outcomes are:

H   H H

T   HT

H   TH

T   TT

Using any of these methods of recording the possible outcomes, we can see that there are *four* possible outcomes: HH, HT, TH, TT. Of course when we are tossing the two coins at the same time, we cannot tell the difference between an HT and a TH. From these diagrams it is possible to deduce that the probability of tossing two heads is $\frac{1}{4}$, the probability of tossing two tails is $\frac{1}{4}$ and the probability of tossing a head and a tail (or a tail and a head) is $\frac{2}{4}$ or $\frac{1}{2}$. All these probabilities add up to I.

We can explain these probabilities in another way. We already know that the probability of tossing a head or a tail on *one* coin is $\frac{1}{2}$. We use this information in order to work out the probability of the possible outcomes of tossing two coins:

The probability of tossing two heads (a head and a head) =

$$P(H) \times P(H) = \tfrac{1}{2} \times \tfrac{1}{2} = \tfrac{1}{4}$$

The probability of tossing two tails (a tail and a tail) =

$$P(T) \times P(T) = \tfrac{1}{2} \times \tfrac{1}{2} = \tfrac{1}{4}$$

When two *independent* events (A & B) occur, then the probability that A and B will *both* happen is:

$$P(A \text{ and } B) = P(A) \times P(B)$$

Now the same rule follows for tossing a head and a tail (or a tail and a head):

The probability of tossing a head and a tail =

$$P(H) \times P(T) = \tfrac{1}{2} \times \tfrac{1}{2} = \tfrac{1}{4}$$

or

The probability of tossing a tail and a head =

$$P(T) \times P(H) = \tfrac{1}{2} \times \tfrac{1}{2} = \tfrac{1}{4}$$

But, because these two possible outcomes look the same when the coins are tossed, we can add the probabilities together:

$$P(H \text{ and } T) \text{ or } P(T \text{ and } H) = \tfrac{1}{4} + \tfrac{1}{4} = \tfrac{2}{4} = \tfrac{1}{2}$$

Think about this

A game for children requires them to place ten counters anywhere they choose along a number track from 2 to 12:

2	3	4	5	6	7	8	9	10	11	12

The children then take turns to roll two dice, adding the totals on the dice. If the square with the sum on it has a counter, the child can remove it. The winner is the child who is first to remove all their counters.

The children place their counters on their favourite numbers, and get frustrated when they cannot throw some of the numbers at the extremes of the number track very often.

What knowledge do you need in order to explain this to your pupils?

Using a systematic method of recording, we can look at all the ways it is possible to throw each of the sums:

Sum	Possible throws (dice 1 + dice 2)	No. of possible ways to make the sum	Probability of throwing the sum
2	1 + 1	1	$\frac{1}{36}$
3	1 + 2, 2 + 1	2	$\frac{2}{36} = \frac{1}{18}$
4	1 + 3, 2 + 2, 3 + 1	3	$\frac{3}{36} = \frac{1}{12}$
5	1 + 4, 2 + 3, 3 + 2, 4 + 1	4	$\frac{4}{36} = \frac{1}{9}$
6	1 + 5, 2 + 4, 3 + 3, 4 + 2, 5 + 1	5	$\frac{5}{36}$
7	1 + 6, 2 + 5, 3 + 4, 4 + 3, 5 + 2, 6 + 1	6	$\frac{6}{36} = \frac{1}{6}$
8	2 + 6, 3 + 5, 4 + 4, 5 + 3, 6 + 2	5	$\frac{5}{36}$
9	3 + 6, 4 + 5, 5 + 4, 3 + 6	4	$\frac{4}{36} = \frac{1}{9}$
10	4 + 6, 5 + 5, 6 + 4	3	$\frac{3}{36} = \frac{1}{12}$
11	5 + 6, 6 + 5	2	$\frac{2}{36} = \frac{1}{18}$
12	6 + 6	1	$\frac{1}{36}$
		36	1

We can see from this chart that the number that is most likely to be thrown is 7 and the numbers that are least likely to be thrown are 2 and 12.

It is possible to use a two-way table to demonstrate this as well:

				Die 2			
	+	1	2	3	4	5	6
Die 1	1	2	3	4	5	6	7
	2	3	4	5	6	7	8
	3	4	5	6	7	8	9
	4	5	6	7	8	9	10
	5	6	7	8	9	10	11
	6	7	8	9	10	11	12

Think about this

You have explained to the children all the ways it is possible to throw each of the sums and you think they understand the probability of throwing the different totals.

The next time they play, some of the children put all ten of their counters on the number seven and then get despondent when they do not win.

What knowledge do you need in order to explain to them why they were not likely to win?

Although 7 is the most likely number to be thrown ($P(7) = \frac{1}{6}$), the probability of throwing a number that was not 7 was much higher ($P(\text{not } 7) = \frac{5}{6}$). So those pupils who put all their counters on seven were throwing their dice against the odds!

How would you arrange your ten counters on the number track? Play the game with some friends. Who won? Why? Have another go!

Statistics and Probability:

a summary of key points

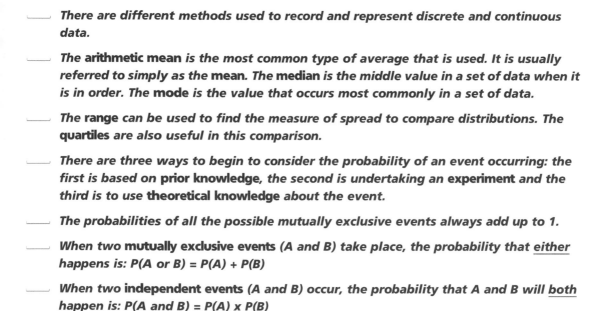

- *Data can be grouped into two categories: **discrete data** (that is collected by counting) and **continuous data** (that is collected by measuring).*

- *There are different methods used to record and represent discrete and continuous data.*

- *The **arithmetic mean** is the most common type of average that is used. It is usually referred to simply as the **mean**. The **median** is the middle value in a set of data when it is in order. The **mode** is the value that occurs most commonly in a set of data.*

- *The **range** can be used to find the measure of spread to compare distributions. The **quartiles** are also useful in this comparison.*

- *There are three ways to begin to consider the probability of an event occurring: the first is based on **prior knowledge**, the second is undertaking an **experiment** and the third is to use **theoretical knowledge** about the event.*

- *The probabilities of all the possible mutually exclusive events always add up to 1.*

- *When two **mutually exclusive events** (A and B) take place, the probability that <u>either</u> happens is: P(A or B) = P(A) + P(B)*

- *When two **independent events** (A and B) occur, the probability that A and B will <u>both</u> happen is: P(A and B) = P(A) x P(B)*

Self-assessment questions

1 Decide whether these groups of data are discrete or continuous:

(a) The number of birds nesting in a field.
(b) The height of trees in a nursery.
(c) The area of towns and cities in England.
(d) The marks of pupils' maths exam paper.

Make up two more examples for both discrete and continuous data.

2 Draw a scattergraph that gives an example of a good positive correlation. What does it mean?

3 The following are two sets of marks from the same group of pupils. The first set is from a maths test and the second from an English test. Both tests were marked out of 20. The marks have been put in order for you.

Maths: 5, 7, 8, 8, 9, 10, 10, 11, 12, 12, 12, 12, 13, 13, 14, 15, 15, 15, 16, 16, 17, 17, 17, 18, 18, 18, 18, 19, 19, 20

English: 3, 5, 5, 7, 8, 8, 9, 9, 10, 10, 10, 10, 11, 12, 12, 13, 13, 14, 14, 14, 14, 14, 15, 15, 16, 17, 17, 17, 18, 19

(a) Which test did the pupils tend to score better in? How do you know?
(b) Calculate the mean, median and mode for each set of data if you have not already done so.
(c) Work out the range and interquartile range for both sets of data.
(d) What reasons might you think explain the difference in test scores?

4 Consider the throwing of a regular six-sided die and the tossing of a coin. What is the probability that:

(a) an even number and a head are shown?
(b) a multiple of 3 and a tail are shown?
(c) a 1 and a head are shown?
(d) a multiple of 7 and a head are shown?

Further reading

Haylock, D. (2001) *Mathematics Explained for Primary Teachers*. London: Paul Chapman Publishing. As the title suggests this book explains much of the content of the primary mathematics curriculum. It also addresses key teaching points and gives opportunities to try some self-assessment questions in each area, to further support your subject knowledge development.

Jennings, S. and Dunne, R. (1997) *Mathematics for Primary Teachers: An Audit and Self-Study Guide*. London: Letts Educational. This book allows you to audit your own mathematical subject knowledge, allowing you to identify the areas that you may need extra support in. When you have identified these, the book gives you feedback and strategies as to how you may develop your subject knoweldge.

Williams, E. and Shuard, H. (1997) *Primary Mathematics Today*. Harlow: Longman. This book is a comprehensive text covering all aspects of primary mathematics. It supports subject knowledge development very effectively, while at the same time considering pedagogical issues and clearly detailing progression.

Introduction

Proof is an essential part of the process of doing mathematics. Although mathematics is often perceived as a tidy, well-organised subject, the exploration of mathematical ideas can be quite unstructured and characterised by having hunches, checking, finding oneself up a 'blind alley', trying an alternative strategy and so on. It is at the end of this unpredictable process, when confidence in a generalisation starts to build up, that the aspect of mathematical activity we call proof becomes so important.

Proof is about making certain our ideas are sound. We convince ourselves and justify our results to others. In the classroom, the question, 'How do you know it will always happen?' is a starting point for a proof.

Mathematics can be thought of as being rather like a brick wall; concepts build up on other concepts in a connected structure. Mathematicians like to know this 'wall' is in good shape and the bricks are sound. Proof gives this confidence. It makes mathematics neat and tidy. This is why one great mathematician called proof the 'hygiene' of the subject.

It should be emphasised that proof is by no means the preserve of advanced mathematics. The mathematical thinking of pupils at Key Stage 1 and Key Stage 2 should involve proofs, albeit at appropriate levels of sophistication. This might include justifying ideas by pointing out features on diagrams; the so called informal proofs.

To be able to develop this kind of thinking in the classroom, you first need to understand what is involved in proof. The purpose of the first part of this chapter is to give you this background. The content will also link with aspects of Number, Algebra and Shape elsewhere in this book.

In the second part of the chapter, mathematical language is examined. This includes consideration of the ambiguities in mathematical vocabulary, the development of definitions and mismatches which can occur between language structure and mathematical structure.

2.1b

To achieve QTS you need to have a secure knowledge and understanding of the mathematics content of the National Curriculum for Key Stages 1 and 2 and the methods and expectations set out in the National Numeracy Strategy. For mathematical language, reasoning and proof this includes:

- **mathematical terms which are necessary to enable trainees to be precise in their explanations to pupils, to discuss primary mathematics at a professional level, and to read inspection and classroom-focused research evidence with understanding;**
- **the correct use of =, ≡, ⇒, ∴ ;**
- **the difference between mathematical reasoning and explanation, as well as the proper use of evidence;**
- **following rigorous mathematical argument;**
- **familiarity with methods of proof, including simple deductive proof, proof by exhaustion and disproof by counter-example.**

You may find it helpful to read through the appropriate section of the Handbook that accompanies the Standards for the award of QTS for clarification and support.

Curriculum Guidance for the Foundation Stage, the National Curriculum and the National Numeracy Strategy

Among the key skills in mathematical development, the Curriculum Guidance for the Foundation Stage includes talking about and creating simple patterns. Besides being fundamental to the development of algebra, work with pattern introduces the possibility of encouraging pupils to justify their explanations and predictions. 'Why do you think we need this shape next?'

In the Mathematics National Curriculum the Programmes of Study clearly state the knowledge, skills and understanding which are to be taught throughout the Key Stages. These are closely linked to the Key Objectives identified for each year group within the NNS *Framework for Teaching Mathematics*.

At Key Stage 1 of the National Curriculum (1999) in Using and Applying both Number and also Shape, Space and Measures, there is reference to pupils' explanation and reasoning skills (Ma 2.1i and Ma 3.1f). The importance of these skills as a foundation for proof in later Key Stages is emphasised.

In Key Stage 2, ability to explain and justify reasoning is taken further and also includes the requirement to develop logical thinking (Ma 2.1k, Ma 3.1h and Ma 4.1h). These aspects of mathematical thinking are echoed in the Teaching Programmes of the NNS *Framework* relating to Reasoning About Numbers and Shape. Pupils might be asked to explain why the 100th term of a number pattern must be a particular value (without, of course, counting all the way up from, say, the 8th term). They could also explore the logical consequences of definitions, such as 'Triangles with two equal sides' and 'Triangles with only two equal sides'.

Within the examples from number, shape and measure, there are countless opportunities to develop the idea of proof and the logical thinking which underpins it.

Levels of proof

Consider how two groups of primary school pupils approached thinking about what happens when we add two odd numbers together.

A group of six-year-olds were adding lots of pairs of odd numbers and getting mostly the right answers which they saw were even. After several pages of calculations had been done, the teacher asked the pupils if they thought the answer would always be even, whichever two odd numbers were added together. The essence of their response was to point to the many calculations showing *odd + odd = even* and to volunteer to do a few extra ones for good measure. They were utterly convinced. It had worked about thirty times so it would always happen!

In the second classroom where the pupils were a little older, the teacher was promoting discussion through the use of a picture to model odd and even numbers. Even numbers were represented by pairs of friends holding hands while odd numbers were shown as pairs of friends plus one individual standing alone.

Even   Odd

After some practice making pictures of various odd and even numbers, the teacher led discussion on to what would happen if two odd numbers were added. Pupils quickly saw that the two unattached children at the end of each line would be able to pair up, thus giving an even number. What is more, it became clear to pupils that however far the pairs of these odd numbers stretched, the result of putting them together would always be an even number.

Notice the different levels of mathematical thinking in each of these scenarios. In the first example, pupils are arriving at a generalised rule by trying out a few examples. This type of thinking is known as **induction**. The limitation of the approach is that we can never be sure that the examples we have *not* tried will conform to this rule. The history of mathematics is littered with mathematicians' hunches (conjectures) based upon inductive thinking which eventually were shown to be false. An example of this is this pattern of numbers:

$$31 \quad 331 \quad 3331 \quad 33331 \quad 333331 \quad 3333331 \quad 33333331$$

Mathematicians knew that the first seven numbers in this pattern were prime (only divisible by one and themselves). They also believed that however long the pattern was continued, the resulting number would be prime. It came as a salutary lesson about the limitations of inductive reasoning when it was discovered that $33333331 = 17 \times 19607843$ and was therefore not prime!

While inductive thinking can often open up exciting possibilities by showing possible relationships, it can never be a guarantee of the validity of these relationships.

Let us now return to the second classroom example. Notice here that the mathematical reasoning is at a much more powerful level. Despite the childish nature of the representation, there was an attempt to justify the general case of addition of **any two** odd numbers. In fact, this 'picture proof' is only a short step from a sophisticated algebraic approach. You might find it helpful to reflect on the correspondence between the algebraic proof below and the reasoning based on the pictures.

Proof that the sum of two odd numbers is even:

We can write an even number as $2a$, where a is an integer. Similarly, an odd number can be written as $2a + 1$. (For example, the odd number 17 is twice 8 plus 1.)

Our two odd numbers could then be $2a + 1$ and $2b + 1$.

Adding, we have $\quad 2a + 1 + 2b + 1$
$$= 2a + 2b + 2$$
$$= 2(a + b + 1)$$

Now $a + b + 1$ is an integer and this implies that $2(a + b + 1)$ is even. Therefore the sum of two odd numbers is even.

(Note that 'implies' and 'therefore' could be represented by the symbols $\Rightarrow$ and $\therefore$ respectively.)

The nub of the argument, in more accessible language, is that $2(a + b + 1)$ is twice some whole number and so must be even.

At this point you may feel confident enough to write an algebraic proof that the sum of two **even** numbers is even.

We have seen how a simple rule about adding two odd numbers can be justified at different levels ranging from the unsatisfactory inductive approach to the formal algebraic method. This last method is an example of what we call a **deductive proof**. It is effective because, by representing odd and even numbers in a generalised, algebraic way, we are taking into account the sum of *all* possible pairs of odd numbers.

Next, we take a more detailed look at deductive proof.

Deductive proof

The proof of the *odd + odd = even* example which we have just considered is characterised by a series of steps. Each step can be **deduced** from the one before. There are also some **assumptions** we have made, for example, about the nature of odd and even numbers. We could use the analogy of a ladder to think about deductive proof.

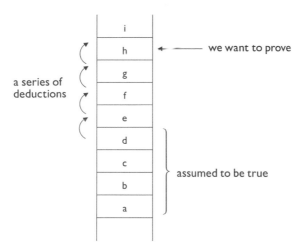

Suppose we want to prove 'idea h' starting from 'idea d'. In starting on rung d, we are taking for granted the ideas a, b, c and d. These have already been proved. They are assumptions. Next we need to logically justify each step up from d to h. It can be thought of as an 'if… then …' process. If d is true, then e must be true; if e is true, then f must be true and so on, finally arriving at 'idea h', which is then proved.

Here is an example of this process in a geometric context:

Proof that the exterior angle of a triangle is equal to the sum of the interior opposite angles:

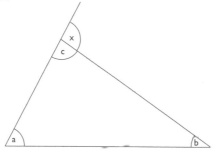

We are trying to prove that, for any triangle, $\hat{x} = \hat{a} + \hat{b}$

We know that $\quad\quad \hat{c} + \hat{x} = 180°$ (a straight angle)
Also, $\quad\quad\quad \hat{c} + \hat{a} + \hat{b} = 180°$ (sum of angles of a triangle)
$\quad\quad\quad \Rightarrow \hat{c} + \hat{x} = \hat{c} + \hat{a} + \hat{b}$
$\quad\quad\quad \therefore \quad \hat{x} = \hat{a} + \hat{b}$

In this short **theorem**, as geometric proofs are sometimes referred to, we have made some assumptions. It is taken for granted that the sum of the interior angles of a triangle is 180°, and that a straight angle is 180°. Someone else has already proved this. Also, we take as self-evident the rules for manipulating algebraic symbols. From this position on our ladder, we are only two short steps away from our required proof.

Pupils in primary school are often introduced to the sum of the interior angles of a triangle through the practical exercise of tearing off the angles from paper triangles and fitting these angles together to make half a rotation.

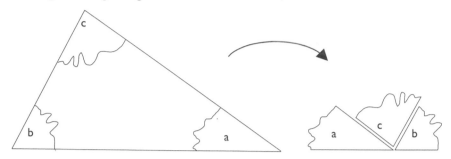

Although the activity lends support to the idea that the sum of the angles might well be 180°, it is not in itself an adequate proof.

Proof that the sum of the interior angles of a triangle is 180°:

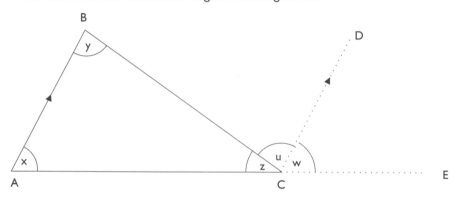

Extend AC to E and draw CD parallel to AB

$\hat{x} = \hat{w}$ (corresponding angles on parallels AB and CD)

$\hat{y} = \hat{u}$ (alternate angles on parallels AB and CD)

 For more information on angles on parallel lines see page 72 in the measures chapter.

Now $\hat{z} + \hat{u} + \hat{w} = 180°$ (straight angle)

Replacing $\hat{u} + \hat{w}$ with $\hat{x} + \hat{y}$,

we have $\hat{z} + \hat{x} + \hat{y} = 180°$

Hence the sum of the interior angles of a triangle is 180°

Notice that we are again starting from assumptions, one of which is about the relationship between angles produced when a pair of parallel lines intersects with a third line.

It is interesting to reflect upon the fleeting nature of fame. How many of the names of today's celebrities will have a familiar ring even fifty years from now? In contrast, the Greek mathematician Pythagoras, who lived in the sixth century BC, has achieved enduring fame

Pythagoras' theorem states that if the length of the hypotenuse is squared this is equal to the sum of the squares of the lengths of the two other sides.

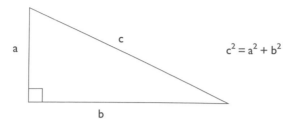

$$c^2 = a^2 + b^2$$

There are many proofs of Pythagoras' theorem and this is one of the more accessible ones. We start from the assumption that the inner shape shown below is a square. This is, in fact, relatively easy to show using the angles of the four right-angled triangles. Also, note that the area of each of the right-angled triangles is $\frac{1}{2}ab$.

 For more information on Pythagoras' Theorem, see page 80 of the shape and space chapter.

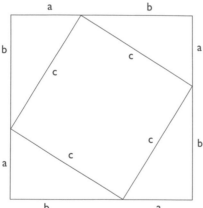

The total area of the large square is $(a + b)^2$. But this is equal to the sum of the area of the inner square plus the area of the four right-angled triangles which is $c^2 + 4(\frac{1}{2}ab)$.

Putting these expressions equal to each other gives

$$(a + b)^2 = c^2 + 4(\tfrac{1}{2}ab)$$

Multiplying out the brackets gives

$$a^2 + 2ab + b^2 = c^2 + 2ab$$

Subtracting 2ab from each sides results in

$$a^2 + b^2 = c^2 \quad \text{(Pythagoras' relationship)}$$

The Greek mathematician Euclid lived 250 years after Pythagoras. He did mathematics an immense service by collecting together scores of proofs in his *Elements*. One of these proofs states that the angle subtended at the centre of a circle is twice the angle subtended at the circumference.

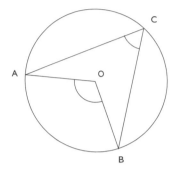

You might like to have a go at proving that $A\hat{O}B = 2A\hat{C}B$ before reading further. You should start by drawing a diameter-line through OC.

If AO, CO and BO are radii, then triangles AOC and BOC are isosceles.

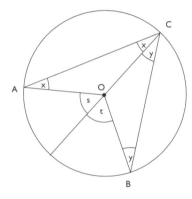

These isosceles triangles have equal base angles which we can label $\hat{x}$ and $\hat{y}$.

Now $\hat{s} = 2\hat{x}$ (exterior angle equal to sum of interior opposite angles)
and $\hat{t} = 2\hat{y}$
hence $\hat{s} + \hat{t} = 2\hat{x} + 2\hat{y} = 2(\hat{x} + \hat{y})$
$\hat{s} + \hat{t}$ is the angle at the centre and $\hat{x} + \hat{y}$ is the angle at the circumference, so the proof is complete.

You might like to consider the implications of this proof if AOB becomes a straight line, i.e. a diameter.

Our last two examples of deductive proof relate to number. Before reading them it would be beneficial to attempt to prove the results yourself.

Proof that prime numbers greater than three either precede or follow a multiple of six.

For example,   16 $\boxed{17}$ 18   30 $\boxed{31}$ 32

Divisible by 6

A prime number greater than 3 is not divisible by 2 and so must be odd.

The two numbers either side of the prime must then be even and are divisible by 2.

Any three consecutive numbers must include at least one number which is divisible by 3. This cannot be the central prime number, so it must be one of the two even numbers on either side.

Hence *one* of the numbers either side of a prime is divisible by both 2 and 3 and is therefore divisible by 6. This completes the proof.

Proof that the sum of three consecutive numbers is divisible by 3:

Three consecutive numbers can be expressed as:

$n, n + 1, n + 2$

Adding, we have:

$n + n + 1 + n + 2$
$= 3n + 3$
$= 3(n + 1)$ which is divisible by 3.

The converse of a proof

It is important to remember that many logical and mathematical statements have a sense of 'direction' about them. As a simple illustration, the statement 'all cats like milk' does not allow us to infer that 'if something likes milk it must be a cat'.

Many proofs or theorems are true in both ways. For example, 'an equilateral triangle has three equal angles' also works in the opposite direction, and it is true that 'a triangle with three equal angles must be an equilateral triangle'. We call this second statement the **converse** of the first.

An example where the converse is not true is the correct statement 'the diagonals of a kite are perpendicular'. The converse of this statement can be easily refuted by using two sheets of tracing paper to show various possible relationships between two perpendicular lines.

Perpendicular diagonals,
but not a kite in sight!

Be on the lookout for proofs for which the converse is false. You might like to consider if the earlier proof that 'the sum of three consecutive numbers is divisible by 3' has a converse.

 For more information on these laws, see page 9 for the section on laws of arithmetic.

The steps of an algebraic proof, in which symbols are added and multiplied then regrouped, are based upon the fundamental laws of arithmetic, which we assume to be true. These laws include the **commutative**, **associative** and **distributive relationships** and rules about inverses. For example, we take for granted that $2a + 2b$ can be changed to $2(a + b)$. When we switch on our 'rules of algebra auto-pilot', some interesting consequences emerge.

It is easy to make a plausible case for the answer to $+2 \times -3$. Writing two cheques each for £3 results in a debit of £6, i.e. -6. In a similar way, the calculation could have been modelled using two temperature reductions of three degrees each. Why is it then that $-2 \times -3 = +6$? More support is needed than the famous 'two minuses make a plus', and students often find it perplexing that there is no helpful everyday justification for this result. This is the reason why the answer to $-2 \times -3 = +6$ is found in the rules of arithmetic, rather than our everyday world.

Let us assume the result $+2 \times -3 = -6$ (we could prove this in a similar way)

Let $-2 \times -3 = y$

adding $+2 \times -3$ to each side we have:

$$+2 \times -3 + -2 \times -3 = +2 \times -3 + y$$

factorising the left-hand side gives:

$$-3(+2 + -2) = +2 \times -3 + y$$
so $\qquad -3(0) = -6 + y$
and $\qquad 0 = -6 + y$
$\therefore \qquad y = +6$

If the rules of arithmetic are consistent for both positive and negative numbers, then -2×-3 *must* equal $+6$.

We now move on to consider two other types of proof which are part of a mathematician's armoury.

Disproof by counter-example

An advantage of this type of proof is that it is usually much easier to prove something is not true than prove that it is true. The statement 'all Englishmen like cricket' would be extremely difficult to verify. Even if we had knocked on every door in the land and all the replies had been affirmative, there would still be a niggling doubt that we might have missed someone. To disprove this assertion would only require one Englishman to say he did not like cricket. It might take a while to find him but, once done, the disproof would be complete.

Our 'Englishman who does not like cricket' is known as a **counter-example**. Finding counter-examples is a powerful way of disproving assertions and is a useful technique for encouraging pupils to reflect on misconceptions.

An example of such an interaction might be:

(Teacher)	Tell me how you know if a shape is a square.
(Pupil)	It has got four sides all the same length.
(T)	So this is a square then. ◇
(P)	Oh, it's not ...

Here is a geometric example of the use of counter-example. The figure below shows various numbers of dots marked on the circumference of circles and joined up to form regions.

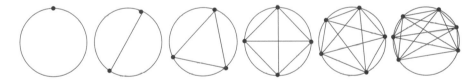

Counting the regions in the first four circles gives the numbers 1, 2, 4 and 8. At this point a mathematician's pulse starts to race a little. Will the next circle have 16 regions? Sure enough it has. Excitement really sets in as the regions are counted for the sixth circle. Hopes are dashed though, as recounting verifies that the number of regions is in fact 31 and not the expected 32. This is the counter-example which proves that we are not dealing with a simple doubling relationship. In fact the formula relating dots and regions is as follows:

$$\tfrac{1}{24}(n^4 - 6n^3 + 23n^2 - 18n + 24)$$

'When a number is multiplied by 10, a nought is added' is a commonly generalised rule. It is true for multiplying whole numbers by ten, but a counter-example such as 0.2×10 highlights its limited validity.

In the context of measurement, younger pupils frequently make a generalisation based on their experience that bigger objects are heavier than smaller objects. It seems quite reasonable to them as, after all, footballs are heavier than tennis balls. A large block of polystyrene is an appropriate counter-example to demolish this incorrect assertion.

We have seen how counter-examples are not only important in refuting incorrect conjectures, but can also be a powerful teaching strategy for encouraging pupils to reflect upon and refine their mathematical beliefs.

There is an old adage: the exception proves the rule. In mathematics, however, it is the exception which disproves the rule!

Practical task

This classroom example provides pupils with an opportunity to appreciate the value of counter-examples.

One pupil devises a rule which is kept secret from the others in the group. They are, however, given one example which fits the rule. This could be, for example:

7 5 3 1

The group then tries to discover the secret rule by suggesting other examples, which receive the answer yes or no according to whether they fit or not.

There are many possible rules which could accommodate this particular, four-digit sequence. Here are some of them:

a) a descending list of consecutive, odd numbers;

b) a descending list of odd numbers;

c) any four digit list;

d) a number less thon 10000;

e) a list of four or less odd digits.

Suppose the secret rule chosen was e). Which examples would help the group 'home in' on it? Clearly 9 7 5 3 would not provide a counter-example for any of the rules a) to e). Suggesting 5 3 1 though would enable c) to be rejected. Certainly 1 9 7 would be a useful example to present. Why?

A key aspect of this game is to encourage pupils to choose their counter-examples carefully.

Proof by exhaustion

The general proofs considered earlier in this chapter take into account the infinite nature of our number system and the countless number of shapes which could be drawn. These proofs ensure we do not have to check, one by one, all the possible pairs of odd numbers or all the different types of triangles. Indeed, this would be impossible, not because of the time factor or effort involved, but in principle.

There are, however, occasions when a convincing proof can be arrived at by considering all the possibilities. This approach is known as **proof by exhaustion**. Here are some examples.

Proof that there are **8** possible outcomes if you toss a coin three times:

This can be shown easily with the help of a tree diagram:

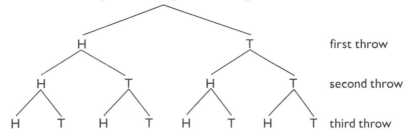

first throw

second throw

third throw

Following every route from top to bottom gives the **8** possibilities.

The following activity involves combining moves about a network. The four moves are horizontal (H), vertical (V), diagonal (D) and no move (N). We always start or finish on a corner of the rectangle.

Proof that if we 'add' any pair of moves the system is closed (i.e. we only get answers which are in the original set of moves):

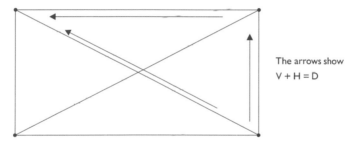

The arrows show

V + H = D

The possibilities can be exhausted by setting out an 'addition' table where V + H means, 'V followed by H'.

+	N	H	V	D
N	N	H	V	D
H	H	N	D	V
V	V	D	N	H
D	D	V	H	N

It can be seen that the addition of any pair of moves results in one of the four original moves. The symmetry of the network makes it irrelevant which corner we start from.

(This is an example of what is known in mathematics as a **finite group**.)

It is important, when exhausting possibilities, to work systematically. Pupils, left to their own devices, frequently work in a haphazard manner which can result in omissions. They are left wondering, 'Have I got them all?'

The next example requires an exhaustive search.

Proof that 6 different tiles can be made using one colour to shade in the triangles in the following shape:

The first point to note is that there will be some duplicate patterns, for example:

   is the same as

By colouring first none, then one, then two, then three and finally all the triangles, we have the confirmation that the six possibilities are:

Using different shapes, it is possible to devise many variants of this activity. One example would be to start with a 3 by 2 grid and colour various numbers of squares.

Nets which fold up to make solid shapes offer possibilities for exhaustive searches. As you have seen in the chapter on shape and space, there are 11 ways in which six squares can be joined together to form the net of a cube. Finding them requires a systematic approach.

Asking pupils to exhaustively prove they have considered all possibilities involves them in organising and checking their work. This is one of the requirements set out in Using and Applying sections of the Mathematics National Curriculum.

Not all exhaustive methods are as straightforward as finding the nets of a cube. In 1852 a mathematician, Francis Guthrie, was colouring in a map showing the counties of England, when it occurred to him that there might be a rule for the minimum number of colours required for any map, so that the same colour was not used on either side of a common border. He found he only needed four colours. For over a hundred years no one could find a map that needed more then four colours, yet mathematicians were unable to prove this. It became known as the **four colour problem**. In 1976, Haken and Appel reduced the problem to 1482 basic configurations and used a computer to check all the combinations within these maps. After 1200 hours of computer running time, it was found that none had required more than four colours. This so-called 'silicon proof' caused consternation amongst some mathematicians because it was humanly impossible to check what had taken a computer so long to do; on the other hand, they were reluctant to take the result on trust from a machine!

Knowledge of the following two types of proof is not essential for QTS status. They are included for interest and also to give a more complete overview of this important aspect of mathematical activity.

Reductio ad absurdum

This type of proof involves assuming that an idea which is in doubt is actually true. Working with this assumed truth, a contradiction arises which confirms the original belief. The easiest approach to understanding this is through an example.

It is interesting to ask adults and children the answer to dividing a number by zero, e.g. $6 \div 0$. Answers such as 0, 6 or even infinity (note there is no number called infinity!) are sometimes given. Younger pupils often reason along the lines, 'There are 6 sweets and nobody is there to share them, so there will be 6 left.' The correct answer to this problem is that it is impossible to divide by zero. If we try, contradictions emerge.

Proof that we cannot divide by zero:

Let us assume that division by zero is possible. The consequence of this is that zero must behave like other numbers, e.g.:

$$1 \div 1 = 1, \quad 5 \div 5 = 1, \quad 37 \div 37 = 1, \quad x \div x = 1 \quad \text{so} \quad 0 \div 0 = 1$$

Now $2 \times 0 = 3 \times 0 = 0$

Dividing by zero gives:

$$\frac{2 \times 0}{0} = \frac{3 \times 0}{0}$$

Cancelling the zeros,

$$\frac{2 \times \cancel{0}}{\cancel{0}} = \frac{3 \times \cancel{0}}{\cancel{0}}$$

$$\therefore \quad 2 = 3 !$$

This is clearly absurd. Hence we cannot divide by zero.

Euclid used this sophisticated technique to prove the existence of the irrational numbers.

Proof by induction

This technique should not be confused with inductive thinking, in which generalisations are made from a limited number of examples.

One way of arriving at a plausible rule for the sum of the first n, natural numbers, is to take the list, reverse it and add the two together:

For example:

$$
\begin{array}{r}
1 + 2 + 3 + 4 \\
+\ 4 + 3 + 2 + 1 \\
\hline
5 + 5 + 5 + 5
\end{array}
\qquad
\begin{array}{r}
1 + 2 + 3 + 4 + 5 + 6 \\
+\ 6 + 5 + 4 + 3 + 2 + 1 \\
\hline
7 + 7 + 7 + 7 + 7 + 7
\end{array}
$$

Finally, we halve each total and arrive at the sum:

$$\frac{4 \times 5}{2} = 10 \ \text{ and } \ \frac{6 \times 7}{2} = 21$$

Doing this for several lists suggests the formula:

$$\tfrac{1}{2}n(n + 1)$$

We can check that this formula works for particular lists, but how can we be sure it must always give the correct sum, however long the list of numbers?

The following analogy will help convey a sense of what is involved in this proof. An interesting spectacle is provided by lining up, in patterns, hundreds of dominoes with each one standing on its end. The first domino can be pushed over which starts a ripple travelling down the line until the last shape falls over. If it were possible to line up an infinite number of dominoes, this ripple would go on for ever. What conditions would ensure that all the dominoes go over?

(1) If any domino falls, the one after it must fall.

(2) The first domino falls over.

These two conditions are the basis of proof by induction.

Proof that the formula for the first n, natural numbers is given by

$$\tfrac{1}{2}n(n + 1)$$

We first assume the formula is true for n and demonstrate that it must therefore be true for n + 1. This is equivalent to changing the above formula to:

$$\tfrac{1}{2}(n + 1)[(n + 1) + 1]$$

(Like going from $\tfrac{1}{2}$ of 6 × 7 to $\tfrac{1}{2}$ of 7 × 8.)

Assume sum(n) = $\tfrac{1}{2}$n(n + 1)

Then sum(n + 1) = sum(n) + (n + 1)

sum(n + 1) = $\tfrac{1}{2}$n(n + 1) + (n + 1)

Rearranging and regrouping gives:

$$\text{sum}(n + 1) = \frac{n(n+1) + 2(n+1)}{2}$$

$$= \tfrac{1}{2}(n + 1)(n + 2)$$

$$\therefore \quad \text{sum}(n + 1) = \tfrac{1}{2}(n + 1)[(n + 1) + 1]$$

Note that this is the original formula with n + 1 replacing n. We have shown condition (1) applies.

Finally, all we have to address is condition (2), that the formula works for the first natural number, one.

$$\text{sum}(1) = \tfrac{1}{2}.1.(1 + 1) = 1 \quad \text{completing the proof}$$

So, the first domino falls over and the rest follow one by one for ever.

Mathematical proof versus scientific theories

Mathematicians have devised sophisticated techniques of proof to underpin their ideas with certainty. Starting from assumptions, the truth of which has been established, they argue step by step to a new conclusion. If the argument is logically sound, then the conclusion is established for all time. The theorems of Euclid and Pythagoras are as true today as they were 2000 years ago and another two millennia are unlikely to dent their validity.

This is not the case with scientific theories which are the poor relations of mathematical proofs. In science, hypotheses are suggested as likely explanations of the physical world. If the hypothesis is sound, then further observations will strengthen our belief in it. The hypothesis enables us to make predictions which can be tested and further increase our confidence. As more and more evidence accumulates, our confidence in the hypothesis reaches the point where it becomes known as a theory.

Theories, however, unlike proofs, have a potential 'shelf life' and are the best explanations of the world only until someone comes along with a better idea. Theories are subjected to the evolutionary pressures of competition and only the fittest survive. There is an enormous graveyard of scientific theories, including some which, in their time, were outstanding. Even Newton's towering achievements have been found inadequate to explain what happens at extremes of size and velocity. Quantum physics and Einstein's General Theory of Relativity have taken over as better explanations of what happens at sub-atomic levels and in the depths of our universe.

The four colour problem was an indication that mathematical proofs can be long and intractable. Perhaps the most famous example of a difficult proof is the one originating with Pierre de Fermat. It came to be known as **Fermat's Last Theorem**.

For more information on Pythagorean triples, see page 80 for the section on Pythagoras' Theorem.

Fermat, who lived in France in the seventeenth century, was a prodigiously talented mathematician. The starting point of his theorem was the whole-number solutions to Pythagoras' Theorem, the so-called **Pythagorean triples**, examples of which are:

$$3, 4, 5 \quad (3^2 + 4^2 = 5^2) \quad \text{and} \quad 5, 12, 13 \quad (5^2 + 12^2 = 13^2)$$

These examples demonstrate that there are whole numbers, a, b and c which satisfy the equation:

$$a^2 + b^2 = c^2$$

Fermat then pondered whether there might be whole number solutions for higher powers of a, b and c in equations such as:

$$a^3 + b^3 = c^3$$
$$\text{and} \quad a^4 + b^4 = c^4$$

Although it was known that there are an infinite number of Pythagorean triples, no solutions to the equations for higher powers of a, b and c could be found. After Fermat's death, his collected notes indicated that he had devised a short proof that there were no whole-number solutions for $z > 2$ for the equation:

$$a^z + b^z = c^z$$

Unfortunately, this proof never came to light and the problem has tantalised mathematicians for 350 years. Although it kept the title of 'theorem', it should really have been known as Fermat's Conjecture, as no proof was available. Finally, in 1995, after numerous attempts by mathematicians over many years, Andrew Wiles of Cambridge solved Fermat's Last Theorem. Whether Fermat did devise a short, valid proof is uncertain. It could be an interesting case of achieving lasting fame for failing to prove a theorem!

Language in mathematics

A cursory glance at the language of mathematics confirms there are many potential difficulties and ambiguities. Even the most exotic of flowers is unlikely to have a square root, while 'take-aways' in the mathematics classroom do not usually come topped with pepperoni! In this section we explore some of these issues.

The concepts which are the building bricks of mathematics are abstract and therefore lacking physical reality. We can have three chairs, three biscuits and three pencils. These can be seen and touched. Three on its own, however, has no concrete reality. It is a generalisation. In order to think about mathematics ourselves and talk about it with others, we need a means of representing these subtle and often difficult ideas.

There are three ways in which we can represent mathematical ideas:

First, they can be described using words, phrases and sentences. For example, 'quadrilateral', 'which are factors of 12' and 'multiply each side of the equation by 3' each say something mathematical.

The second representation is through the use of pictures and objects which can be a valuable aid to understanding. Younger pupils particularly benefit from representations such as **number lines** and **tens/units apparatus**. These help develop images which can then be internalised. There is a saying that a picture paints a thousand words and many students find, for example, the grid representation of long multiplication, very helpful in clarifying understanding. Though these concrete props are useful, the NNS makes the important point that mathematics is a mental activity, and pupils should not be using apparatus indiscriminately once understanding has become secure. A problem can arise when certain representations are exclusively linked with particular aspects of mathematics. For example, it is sometimes forgotten that fractions should appear on the number line and not just as parts of circles or squares.

Third, and most challenging for pupils, is the use of symbols to represent mathematics. Because of their abstract nature, symbols are introduced after the use of language and pictorial representation. The premature introduction of symbolism can be a barrier to understanding and confidence. It would be impossible to develop mathematically without familiarity with symbols, and teachers have to make fine judgements about the right moment to take this step. The relationship between these three representations of mathematical ideas can be shown as:

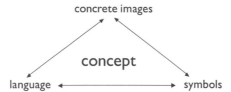

For example, taking the idea of place value, there could be links between:

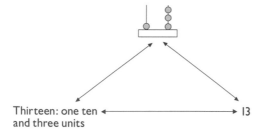

The remainder of this chapter will focus upon the use of language to describe mathematical ideas.

Vocabulary

Difficult mathematical language has tended to be pruned from the curriculum over recent years and few pupils have to grapple with words like *subtrahend* and *quotient*.

There is, however, a basic repertoire of precise terms which are a necessary part of mathematical education. Terms such as *numerator* and *denominator* need to be learned. Descriptions such as 'the number at the top' are not only more complicated but also vague and apply to a range of very different mathematical examples. A well-meaning but misguided tendency to avoid what are considered difficult words also fails to take into account that these terms are no more complicated than words such as refrigerator or computer.

Besides technical terms, used exclusively within a mathematical context, there are many words which have a meaning both within mathematics and also in everyday usage. Sometimes the everyday meaning coincides with the mathematical meaning, but on other occasions the meanings are quite different, causing problems for pupils. Kane, in 1967, coined the terms *Ordinary English (OE)* and *Mathematical English (ME)* to draw attention to the complex interplay between language and mathematics. The table below shows examples of these different categories:

ME same as OE	ME different from OE	A ME meaning only
Price	Difference	Equilateral
Twelve	Match	Isosceles
Wide	Odd	Parallelogram
Cube	Mean	Numerator
Oblong	Power	Hypotenuse
Vertical	Table	Rhombus
Clockwise	Volume	Subtract
	Product	Congruent
	Cancel	
	Factor	

Perhaps you can think of other vocabulary to add to these lists.

Words with just a mathematical meaning can be difficult for pupils. Much of this vocabulary has Latin and Greek origins and pupils are unlikely to have any background from which useful connections can be made. Another factor is that pupils simply do not hear these words frequently enough in context, and so familiarity is slow to develop.

Words which have different meanings in OE and ME cause much confusion and it is often only by probing that these difficulties come to light. The attempt by pupils to make sense of wrong meanings such as odd (peculiar) numbers is both interesting and illuminating. A lovely example is given by Hobart (1980) where a secondary pupil has difficulty with a question starting 'What is common to …?' The problem arose because of an association between 'common' and 'too much lipstick'!

In order to avoid ambiguity and develop correct terminology, it is important that teachers are aware of the need to discuss these differences in meaning. Straker (1993) stresses the need to extend informal vocabulary by gradually refining terms to give more precise meaning. Each child should trace steps from the familiar to the new. The implication here is that there should be progression in the development of mathematical language and this should be reflected in school planning. In sorting out a suitable order in which to introduce mathematical concepts, it is easy to forget that the development of language such as:

three fours, three times four, three lots of four, three multiplied by four, and the product of three and four,

should be in well-planned stages.

Refining definitions

Before focusing on mathematical definitions, it will be helpful to consider how meaning becomes attached to an everyday word like **car**.

Imagine a young child's first encounter with a car: it could be the red mini in the drive. Soon, however, all sorts of other objects are associated with the label 'car'. There is the blue Peugeot next door and the grey Jag across the road. Gradually, many slightly different looking objects are associated with car, even the scale model toys which arrive on birthdays. Alongside this, the child learns about things which are not cars; the machine on two wheels is a bicycle, while the four-wheeled vehicle, which looks like a car with a large matchbox on the back, is not a car but a lorry.

Though a crude simplification, this story illustrates some important points. In learning about a definition, it helps to:

• **associate the definition with different examples – the more varied, the better;**

• **see examples which, though looking vaguely related, do not fit the definition.**

The parents of this hypothetical child do not have to arrange for all the vehicles to pull up outside their house so they can point and say 'car', 'car', 'car', 'lorry', etc. Everyday life will take care of this and the frequent encounters with a variety of 'cars' and 'not cars' will ensure the definition is refined.

The way pupils learn about definitions such as 'triangle' and 'half' could proceed in a similar way, except that everyday life is not littered with a varied range of examples of 'triangles' and 'halves'. Pupils have to rely mainly on teachers and motivated parents to offer this experience. To develop a clear notion of what triangles and halves are, pupils need to experience, over time, triangles of all shapes and sizes and halves that are not limited to straight lines drawn across symmetrical shapes.

As well as examples which match the definitions, counter-examples which hint at inclusion are also of crucial importance. It is by linking vocabulary with carefully chosen examples, that misconceptions can often be avoided.

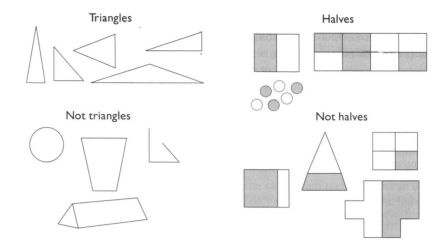

Structure in mathematics and language

Though language patterns and mathematical structure can mirror each other, there are many occasions of mismatch between them. For example, consider the problem:

> There are 16 people at a party. 5 more arrive. How many are there at the party now?

The language pattern corresponds well with the probable method of calculation, in which 5 is added to 16, and also with the symbolic form, $16 + 5 = \square$.

On the other hand, a problem like:

> After putting £6 into my account, I now have £32. How much did I have in my account before this transaction?

shows a much weaker match between the language pattern and the mathematical calculation, $\square + 6 = 32$. Neither the sequencing of the events referred to in the sentence nor the ordering of the numbers corresponds with the standard form of the calculation.

In order to explain the variety of ways of describing addition and subtraction relationships, we can consider the range of problems which involve the numbers 3, 4 and 7:

> What is 3 add 4?
> What is the total of 3 and 4?
> What is 7 take away 3?
> What is the difference between 7 and 4?
> How many more is 7 than 3?
> How many less than 7 is 3?
> If 3 is subtracted from 7 we get?
> What added to 4 makes 7?
> I took 4 from a number and got 3. What was the number?

The connection between these problems and the standard forms for addition and subtraction is far from straightforward. Not surprisingly, younger pupils frequently approach, 'How many more is 7 than 3?', by adding 7 and 3 together to get 10.

Pupils can become familiar with problem patterns by discussing the meaning and representing them in a concrete context such as a number line or money. Varying the numbers in the problem can also be a way of creating 'tension' between the mathematical structure and the language structure. Here is an example:

Problem: What do you add to 18 to get 25?

Pupil   (P): 7
Teacher (T):   How did you do it?
         (P): I counted 19, 20,21,22,23,24,25 that's 7.
         (T): Good. Can you think of another way of working it out?
         (P): No.
         (T): Let's try a different one. What do you add to 2 to get 25?
         (P): 23
         (T): That was quick. Did you count up from 2 to 25?
         (P): No, I took away 2.
         (T): What made you think of doing that?
         (P): Oh, there's two ways, but counting up takes too long.

The key features of this example are that, while the language in the problem encourages a 'count on' approach, the coupling of a very small number with 25 cries out for the subtraction method. This tension results in a new strategy. Note that the problem, 'Twenty-five take away twenty-four', encourages a 'count on' strategy. This approach is extremely valuable in clarifying the inverse relationship.

The number system

There are many inconsistencies in the way the number words are said, causing difficulties for many children. In order to see the irregularities of the English system it is helpful to compare it with the Chinese structure of naming numbers. The Chinese words are translated into English for easy reading.

ENGLISH	CHINESE
One	One
Two	Two
Three	Three
Four	Four
Five	Five
Six	Six
Seven	Seven
Eight	Eight
Nine	Nine
Ten	Ten
Eleven	Ten one
Twelve	Ten two

Thirteen	Ten three
…	…
Eighteen	Ten eight
Nineteen	Ten nine
Twenty	Two ten
Twenty one	Two ten one
Twenty two	Two ten two
…	…
Twenty nine	Two ten nine
Thirty	Three ten
…	…
Eighty	Eight ten
Ninety	Nine ten
One hundred	One hundred
One hundred and one	One hundred one

What is immediately striking about the Chinese system is its regularity. Having learned the first twelve words and 'two ten' it is easy to construct the whole pattern from one to one hundred and beyond. Several Asian languages, including Japanese, have this same logical structure.

The English system has features which make it more difficult to discern the underlying tens—units pattern:

- **the words eleven and twelve do not indicate a 'ten and' composition;**
- **the words 'three' and 'five' are not used again (other than to indicate units), but occur in the form 'thir'(teen) and 'fif'(teen);**
- **in the 'teens' words, the tens and units are reversed (sixteen not teen six);**
- **'teen' and 'ty' both mean ten;**
- **'twenty' does not clearly indicate two tens.**

It is not surprising then that pupils sometimes reverse the digits in 'thirteen'.

Other European languages such as French and German have some of the same problems as our own system. The French system, having roughly matched our own structure to sixteen, suddenly becomes *dix-sept* for seventeen. The later decades are different with 80 being *quatre vingt* (four twenties). The German system has not only the 'teens' reversed but also higher numbers like *vierundzwanzig* (24) which reads like the number words in 'four and twenty blackbirds, baked in a pie.'

The way we say numbers includes several interesting features. 234 is read 'two hundred and thirty four' with the most significant digit (i.e. the hundreds) articulated first. Thompson (1994) found that 87% of pupils preferred to perform addition calculations in the same left-to-right manner, starting with the most significant digit first.

We read large numbers in a variety of different ways. 1066 could be expressed as:

'One thousand and sixty six.'

On the other hand, if the Battle of Hastings was being referred to it would certainly become:

'Ten sixty six.'

Yet again, as a telephone number it might be:

'One, zero, double six.'

When we read a decimal number such as 34.34, the digits following the decimal point are articulated differently to the ones to the left of the point:

'Thirty four point three four.'

Mathematical Language, Reasoning and Proof:
a summary of key points

____ *Proofs are techniques used to convince oneself and others that mathematical ideas are valid. Unlike inductive thinking, which relies upon a limited number of cases, proofs are general and apply to all examples.*

____ *There are several standard methods of proof including:* **deductive proof,** *characterised by logical, step-by-step justification;* **disproof by counter-example,** *in which an argument is refuted by producing a case which does not fit the rule; and* **proof by exhaustion,** *in which all possibilities are checked.*

____ *Mathematics is a hierarchical body of knowledge. At whatever level they are engaged, mathematicians need to know that their work rests on firm foundations. Proof gives this guarantee.*

____ *Proof is important at all stages of mathematics education. Primary school pupils should be taught to reflect upon and justify their reasoning, so laying a foundation for more formal approaches to proof in the later key stages.*

____ *Language is one of three ways of representing mathematics.*

____ *Key mathematical vocabulary is important and pupils need to become familiar with precise terminology.*

____ *Mathematical vocabulary can have a different meaning in Ordinary English. These differences should be made explicit to pupils.*

____ *Pupils' informal vocabulary should be gradually refined into a more precise meaning. Part of this process will involve discussion of well-chosen exemplars.*

____ *Language structure and mathematical structure sometimes do not match well. Pupils need to practice linking verbal problems with familiar contexts. The choice of numbers can affect the way the problem is perceived.*

____ *Our number system has many inconsistencies which can be a hindrance to pupils learning the number names.*

✓ Self-assessment questions

① (a) Prove that the sum of the interior angles of a quadrilateral is always equal to 360°. (You may assume the sum of the angles of a triangle.)

(b) Suggest an approach to this in which pupils use inductive thinking.

② Prove that (a) the product of two even numbers is even, and (b) the product of two odd numbers is odd.

③ Prove that the product of three consecutive numbers is even.

④ Prove by exhaustion that there are only six ways of listing the letters A, B and C.

⑤ Find counter-examples to refute these assertions:

(a) Multiplying makes a number larger.
(b) If a shape has rotational symmetry, it also has reflective symmetry.
(c) If a and b are both factors of x, then either a is a factor of b, or b is a factor of a.

⑥ Prove that for any chord, AB, angles $\hat{a}$ and $\hat{b}$ are equal. List any assumptions you make.

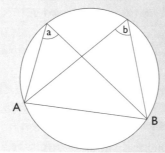

abscissa: the first number in a pair of Cartesian co-ordinates. The abscissa always represents the distance along the x-axis.

angle: a measurement of turn.

approximation: a rough answer.

arc: a curved line that forms part of the circumference of a circle.

associative law: numbers can be regrouped to simplify a question while making no difference to the answer. It is true for addition and multiplication:
$$(a + b) + c = a + (b + c) \quad (a \times b) \times c = a \times (b \times c)$$

average: the general term used for using one number to represent a set of data.

bar graph: a graph that uses bars to represent data.

bar-line graph: a graph that uses lines to represent data.

block graph: a graph used to display discrete data where one block can represent one or many item(s) of data.

BODMAS: the order of precedence given to the operations when working out complex expressions. It stands for:

B – brackets
O – of
D – division
M – multiplication
A – addition
S – subtraction

box and whisker plot: a graphical representation that allows for comparison of two sets of data.

capacity: how much liquid volume a container can hold when full.

Cartesian coordinates: a pair of numbers that locate a point on a plane with reference to two axes (can also refer to three axes in order to locate a point in three dimensions).

commutative law: the order in which the operation is performed makes no difference to the answer. It is true for addition and multiplication:
$$a + b = b + a \quad a \times b = b \times a$$

congruence: shapes are said to be congruent if they are the same shape and size.

conjecture: a hypothesis, something that has been surmised or deduced.

conservation: understanding that the quantity of matter remains unchanged regardless of its arrangement.

continuous data: data that is measured. Every item of data can be placed along a continuum, for example, lengths of leaves.

counter-example: disproving an assertion by finding an exception.

cumulative frequency: a table displaying the running total of a set of data.

cumulative frequency curve: a graph of the running total of a set of data.

data: a set of facts, numbers or information.

decimal: a fractional number expressed using places to the right of the decimal point.

deduction: a conclusion based on a set of true statements.

denominator: the bottom digit in a fraction, representing the number of fractional parts the unit has been divided into.

discrete data: data that can be counted. Every item of data can be placed in a category, for example, colours of cars.

distributive law: one operation is 'distributed out' over another operation. It is true for multiplication over addition and multiplication over subtraction:

$$a \times (b + c) = (a \times b) + (a \times c) \qquad a \times (b - c) = (a \times b) - (a \times c)$$

It is also true that division is 'right distributive' over addition and subtraction (i.e. the division needs to be on the right side of the brackets):

$$(a + b) \div c = (a \div c) + (b \div c) \qquad (a - b) \div c = (a \div c) - (b \div c)$$

dividend: within the operation of division, the number that is divided by another number.

divisor: within the operation of division, the number that divides another number.

edge: the line where two faces join (i.e. the intersection of two plane faces of a solid).

enlargement: each measurement is multiplied by a scale factor in order to enlarge or reduce an image.

equation: a statement that two expressions are equal.

estimation: the rough answer (a judgement of an approximate value or amount).

exhaustion: a proof that is arrived at by considering all possibilities.

experimental probability: the number between 0 and 1 that is found by dividing the number of outcomes by the total number of trials.

expression: a general term used to describe mathematical terms.

face: the flat surface of a solid shape (i.e. parts of planes).

factor: a number that divides another number exactly, for example 8 is a factor of 32, but 5 is not.

fraction: a fraction is expressed as the quotient of two numbers, the dividend is the numerator, the divisor the denominator.

frequency diagram: a table displaying continuous data grouped into classes.

frequency histogram: a graph displaying continuous data grouped into classes.

function: a rule that changes or maps one number on to another.

gradient: the slope of a graph.

imperial measure: introduced in the Magna Carta in 1215, for example, pints, gallons, miles, etc.

independent events: events when the outcome of one event does not affect the outcome of another event, for example, flipping two coins.

index form: a concise way of writing repeated multiplication of a number by itself, for example, $10 \times 10 \times 10 \times 10 = 10^4$.

inequality: a statement that one quantity is greater or less than another.

interquartile range: the interval between the upper quartile and the lower quartile in a set of data.

irrational numbers: the set of numbers that cannot be expressed in fractional form.

line graph: a graph used to display continuous data, where curves or line segments join points of measured data.

linear equation: takes the form $ay + bx + c = 0$. A linear equation can always be represented as a straight line graph.

lower quartile: the value one quarter of the way along a set of ordered data.

mass: the amount of matter contained in an object.

mean: the sum of the values in a set of data divided by the total number of items in that set.

median: the middle value of a set of ordered data.

minuend: the quantity from which another quantity is to be subtracted.

mode: the value that occurs most often in a set of data.

mutually exclusive events: events which, having happened, exclude any other outcome from occurring in that same event, for example, throwing a 3 on a die excludes a 1, 2, 4, 5 or 6 being thrown at the same time.

net: a flat shape that can be folded to form a solid.

numerator: the top digit in a fraction representing the number of fractional parts.

ordering: putting a collection of items in order from smallest to biggest/biggest to smallest according to weight, length, thickness, etc.

ordinate: the second number in a pair of Cartesian co-ordinates. The ordinate always represents the distance along the y-axis.

parallel: lines travelling in the same direction but which will never meet.

percentage: fractions with a denominator of 100. They can also be represented as decimals, for example $\frac{1}{4} = \frac{25}{100} = 0.25 = 25\%$.

perpendicular: two lines are said to be perpendicular if they meet at right angles.

pi (π): an irrational number found when the circumference of a circle is divided by the diameter. It is approximately equal to 3.141592…

pictograph: a graph used to display discrete data where one picture/symbol can represent one or many item(s) of data.

pie chart: a circle graph cut into sectors.

place value: place value is used by number systems that allow the same digit to carry different values based on its position.

Platonic solids: the five regular polyhedra, comprising the regular tetrahedron, the cube, the regular octahedron, the regular dodecahedron and the regular icosahedron.

polygon: a plane shape with straight sides and many angles.

polyhedron (pl. polyhedra): a solid formed from many flat faces.

prism: a solid shape with a uniform cross section.

probability: used to measure the likelihood of certain events occurring in the future.

probability scale: a scale from 0 to 1 that is used to measure the likelihood of an event occurring, with 0 being impossible and 1 being certain.

proportion: compares part of a quantity with the whole, for example, a ratio of 1:3 results in proportions of 1 out of 4 and 3 out of 4.

pyramid: a solid that has a polygon base and all other faces triangular.

quotient: the result when one number is divided by another number.

range: the interval between the greatest and least values in a set of data.

ratio: a comparison between two quantities.

rational numbers: the set of all numbers that can be written as fractions.

real numbers: the set of rational numbers and irrational numbers combined.

reduction: combining different parts of an equation to make it simpler.

reflection: when a shape is reflected a mirror image is created. The shape and size remain unchanged, the two images are congruent.

reflective symmetry: also sometimes called line symmetry. A shape is said to have reflective symmetry if it can be folded so that one half fits exactly on top of the other half.

restoration: simplifying an equation by performing the same operation on each side.

rotation: rotation involves a turn around a fixed point. The shape and size remain unchanged, the two images are congruent.

rotational symmetry: a shape is said to have rotational symmetry if it looks the same in different positions when rotated about its centre.

scattergraph: a graph representing two types of data plotted as co-ordinates.

sector: a wedge from a circle (like a slice of pie).

sigma: means 'the sum of'. The symbol for sigma is Σ.

similarity: shapes are said to be similar if all the angles are the same size and the shapes are the same but of different size, i.e. one is an enlargement of the other.

simultaneous linear equations: Two linear equations which have a common solution.

standard form: sometimes called standard index form as it uses powers of 10, i.e. 10 expressed in index form. It is a shorthand way of writing very small and very large numbers that would require a huge number of digits if written in full.

statistics: statistics help us to bring order to data and to draw information from it.

subtrahend: the number or term to be subtracted.

Système Internationale (S.I.): determines the units of measurement used in the metric system, for example, millimetres, kilograms, litres, etc.

terms: algebraic quantities that are separated from each other in expressions by operations.

theoretical probability: the number between 0 and 1 that is found by dividing the number of actual outcomes by the total number of possible outcomes.

transitivity: a mathematical relationship used to compare two objects or events, e.g. if A is shorter than B, and B is shorter than C, then A must be shorter than C.

translation: this takes place when a shape is moved from one place to another just by sliding it (without rotating, reflecting or enlarging).

upper quartile: the value three-quarters of the way along a set of ordered data.

vertex: the point of intersection of edges.

volume: the amount of three-dimensional space an object occupies.

weight: the force exerted on a body due to gravity.

y-intercept: the point at which a graph crosses the y-axis.

Chapter 2: Number

(1)

$10 \div 2 + 8 \times 3 - \frac{1}{2} \text{ of } 6 + (4 - 2)$ Brackets

$10 \div 2 + 8 \times 3 - \frac{1}{2} \text{ of } 6 + 2$ Of

$10 \div 2 + 8 \times 3 - 3 + 2$ Division

$\quad\quad 5 \;\; + 8 \times 3 - 3 + 2$ Multiplication

$\quad\quad 5 \;\; + \;\; 24 \;\; - 3 + 2$ Addition

$\quad\quad\quad\quad\quad 31 - 3$ Subtraction

$\quad\quad\quad\quad\quad\quad 28$

(2)   (a) $\frac{7}{14} = \frac{1}{2}$ (b) $\frac{40}{46} = \frac{20}{23}$

     (c) $\frac{121}{187} = \frac{11}{17}$ (d) $\frac{21}{7} = 3$

(3)   (a) $\frac{1}{2} + \frac{5}{7} = \frac{7}{14} + \frac{10}{14} = \frac{17}{14} = 1\frac{3}{14}$

     (b) $\frac{3}{5} + \frac{2}{6} = \frac{18}{30} + \frac{10}{30} = \frac{28}{30} = \frac{14}{15}$

     (c) $\frac{9}{11} - \frac{1}{3} = \frac{27}{33} - \frac{11}{33} = \frac{16}{33}$

     (d) $\frac{3}{4} - \frac{1}{12} = \frac{9}{12} - \frac{1}{12} = \frac{8}{12} = \frac{2}{3}$

     (e) $\frac{1}{5} \times \frac{3}{4} = \frac{3}{20}$

     (f) $\frac{3}{10} \times \frac{1}{9} = \frac{3}{90} = \frac{1}{30}$

     (g) $\frac{1}{9} \div \frac{2}{3} = \frac{1}{9} \times \frac{3}{2} = \frac{3}{18} = \frac{1}{6}$

     (h) $\frac{4}{7} \div \frac{21}{24} = \frac{4}{7} \times \frac{24}{21} = \frac{96}{147} = \frac{32}{49}$

(4)   (a) $\frac{3}{5} = 0.6 = 60\%$ (b) $\frac{7}{10} = 0.7 = 70\%$

     (c) $\frac{1}{8} = 0.125 = 12.5\%$

(5)   (a) $17\frac{1}{2}\%$ of 68 $10\% = 6.8$

                        $5\% = 3.4$

                    $2.5\% = 1.7$

    Thus $17\frac{1}{2}\%$ of $68 = 6.8 + 3.4 + 1.7 = 11.9$

     (b) 75% of 88 $75\% = \frac{3}{4}$

                    $88 \div 4 = 22$

                    $22 \times 3 = 66$

    Thus 75% of $88 = 66$

(c) 60% of 70   10% = 7

          60% = 7 x 6

Thus 60% of 70 = 42

(6) (a) $3x \geqslant 15$ (b) $-3x \geqslant 9$

   $x \geqslant \dfrac{15}{3}$ $x \leqslant \dfrac{9}{-3}$ (don't forget – dividing by a negative

              number reverses the inequality)

   $x \geqslant 5$ $x \leqslant -3$

(c) $4x + 3 < 18$

   $4x \quad < 18 - 3$

   $4x \quad < 15$

   $x \quad < \dfrac{15}{4}$

   $x \quad < 3\frac{3}{4}$

(7) (a) $400 = 4.0 \times 10^2$ (b) $619\,000 = 6.19 \times 10^5$

(c) $8412.3 = 8.4123 \times 10^3$ (d) $0.015 = 1.5 \times 10^{-2}$

(e) $0.000000789 = 7.89 \times 10^{-7}$

Chapter 3: Algebra, Equations, Functions and Graphs

(1) (a) $\quad 5n^2 + 6n - n^2 + 4 - 2n + 1$

   $= 5n^2 - n^2 + 6n - 2n + 4 + 1$

   $= 4n^2 + 4n + 5$

(b) $\quad (pq)^2 + p^2q + 4p^2q^2 - 3p(qp) + pq^2$

   $= p^2q^2 + p^2q + 4p^2q^2 - 3pqp + pq^2$

   $= p^2q^2 + 4p^2q^2 + p^2q - 3ppq + pq^2$

   $= 5p^2q^2 - 2p^2q + pq^2$

(2) (a)   position   1   2   3   4   5

      term   2   5   8   11   14

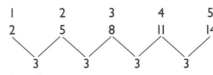

   general term $3n - 1$

(b)   position   1   2   3   4   5

      term   4   8   12   16   20

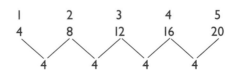

   general term $4n$

3 position (n)

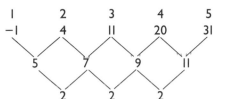

Using $an^2 + bn + c$:

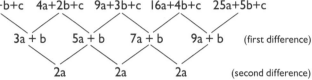

$2a = 2$ so $a = 1$ $\qquad\qquad (n^2 + bn + c)$

Substituting for a in $3a + b = 5$

$\qquad\qquad$ gives $3 + b = 5$

$\qquad\qquad\qquad$ so $b = 5 - 3 = 2$ $\qquad (n^2 + 2n + c)$

Substituting for a and b in $a + b + c = -1$

$\qquad\qquad$ gives $1 + 2 + c = -1$

$\qquad\qquad\qquad$ so $c = -1 - 1 - 2 = -4$

General term $n^2 + 2n - 4$

4 (a) $a - 3b = 1$ $\qquad\qquad$ (1)

$\quad a + 2b = 11$ $\qquad\qquad$ (2)

Subtracting equation (1) from equation (2) gives:

$a + 2b = 11$

$\underline{a - 3b = 1}$

$\quad 5b = 10$

$\qquad b = 2$

Substituting for b in (1) gives:

$a + 2b = 11$

$a + 4 = 11$

$\quad a = 7$

So $a = 7$ and $b = 2$

(b) $2a - 3b = 4$ (1)

     $a + 2b = 9$ (2)

Multiplying equation (2) by 2 gives:

     $2a + 4b = 18$ (3)

Subtracting equation (1) from equation (3) gives:

$$2a + 4b = 18$$
$$\underline{2a - 3b = 4}$$
$$7b = 14$$
$$b = 2$$

Substituting for b in (2) gives:

$$a + 2b = 9$$
$$a + 4 = 9$$
$$a = 5$$

So $a = 5$ and $b = 2$

 (a) $2y = 6x + 4$

This needs to be expressed in the form $y = mx + c$. To do this, every term must be divided by 2, giving:

$y = 3x + 2$

So the gradient is 3 and the y-intercept is 2.

(b) $x + 2y = 4$

This is currently not of the form $y = mx + c$ and therefore needs rearranging:

$$x + 2y = 4$$
$$2y = 4 - x$$
$$2y = (-x) + 4$$
$$y = (-x)/2 + 2$$

So the gradient is $-\frac{1}{2}$ and the y intercept is 2

Chapter 4: Measures

   12 kg

   400 ml

 (a) A is shorter than B. B is shorter than C. Therefore A is shorter than C.

(b) A holds more liquid than B. B holds more liquid than C. Therefore A holds more liquid than C.

(c) A takes less time than B. B takes less time than C. Therefore A takes less time than C.

(4) 23° 62° 87°, $\frac{1}{4}$ turn, 134°, 212°, $\frac{7}{8}$ of a turn (Acute, Acute, Acute, Right, Obtuse, Reflex, Reflex)

Chapter 5: Shape and Space

(1) square, rectangle, parallelogram, rhombus

(2) 12 cm²

(3) 210 cm or 2.1 m

(4) One possible answer for each is shown below:

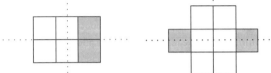

(5) One possible answer for each is shown below:

(6) (a) There are 35 hexominoes. (b) A regular hexahedron.

Chapter 6: Statistics and Probability

(1) (a) discrete (b) continuous (c) continuous (d) discrete

(2) See page 103 for an example of a scattergraph. A good positive correlation describes the tendency that there seems to be a relationship between two sets of data.

(3) (a) Maths. Reasons for choice will vary.

(b) Maths: mean = 13.8   median = 14.5   mode = 12, 18
English: mean = 12   median = 12.5   mode = 14

(c) Maths: range is between 5 and 20
interquartile range is between 10 and 18
English: range is between 3 and 19
interquartile range is between 9 and 15

(d) The only valid statement we can make is that the maths scores were higher than the English scores. It is impossible to tell from the data presented *why* this might be, but some possible reasons could be:

- the English test was harder than the maths test;
- the pupils are better at maths than they are at English;
- the English test was taken in poor conditions; or
- some of the pupils cheated in the maths test!

(4) (a) $\frac{1}{4}$ (b) $\frac{1}{6}$ (c) $\frac{1}{12}$ (d) 0

Chapter 7: Mathematical Language, Reasoning and Proof

(1) (a) A quadrilateral can always be divided into two triangles, e.g.:

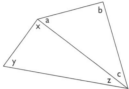

$$(\hat{a} + \hat{b} + \hat{c}) + (\hat{x} + \hat{y} + \hat{z}) = 180° + 180° = 360°$$

But, the four angles of the quadrilateral are also the sum of these six angles.

(b) Pupils could either draw several quadrilaterals, measure the angles and find the sum, or, tear off the corners and show they fit together to make one rotation.

(2) (a) Our two even numbers can be written, 2a and 2b, where a and b are integers. Multiplying gives:

$$2a \times 2b = 2(2ab)$$

2ab is the product of three integers and must also be an integer (an assumption). Hence 2(2ab), the product of two even numbers, must be even.

(b) Writing our odd numbers as 2a + 1 and 2b + 1 and multiplying gives:

$$(2a + 1)(2b + 1) = 4ab + 2b + 2a + 1$$

The final unit makes it impossible to divide this expression by 2, so it is not even. Therefore, the product of two odd numbers is odd.

(3) Three consecutive numbers must contain at least one even number of the form 2a, where a is an integer. The product of 2a and any other two integers gives a number divisible by 2, hence the product is always even.

(4) Undertaken systematically, the possibilities are:

abc bac cab

acb bca cba

(a) $0.1 \times 60 = 6$ or $\frac{1}{2} \times 10 = 5$ would do.

(b) This shape or variations:

(c) 8 and 6 are both factors of 24, but 8 is not a factor of 6 and 6 is not a factor of 8.

6 Assuming the truth of the theorem that the angle subtended at the centre is twice that at the circumference, we can argue:

Let $\hat{x}$ be the angle $A\hat{O}B$, where O is the centre of the circle.

Now $2\hat{a} = \hat{x}$
and $2\hat{b} = \hat{x}$
hence $2\hat{a} = 2\hat{b}$
$\therefore$ $\hat{a} = \hat{b}$

Anghileri, J. (1997) 'Uses of Counting in Multiplication and Division' in I. Thompson (ed.) *Teaching Early Number*. Buckingham: Open University Press.

Atkinson, S. (1992) *Mathematics with Reason*. London: Hodder & Stoughton.

Battista, M. J. (1999) 'The Importance of Spatial Structuring in Geometric Reasoning' in *Teaching Children Mathematics* Vol. 6, No. 3, Nov, pp. 170–77.

Clements, D. H., Swaninathan, S., Zeitler Hannibal, M. A. and Sarama, J. (1999) 'Young Children's Concepts of Shape' in *Journal for Research in Mathematics Education* Vol. 30, No. 2, March, pp. 192–209.

Cockburn, A. (1999) *Teaching Mathematics with Insight: The Identification, Diagnosis and Remediation of Young Children's Mathematical Errors*. London: Falmer Press.

DfEE (1999) *The National Numeracy Strategy: Framework for Teaching Mathematics*. London: DfEE.

DfEE/QCA (1999) *Mathematics: the National Curriculum for England*. London: HMSO.

DfEE (1999) *Mathematical Vocabulary*. DfEE.

Dickson, L., Brown, M. and Gibson, O. (1984) *Children Learning Mathematics: A Teacher's Guide to Recent Research*. London: Cassell Educational Ltd.

Durkin, K. and Shire, B. (eds) (1991) *Language in Mathematical Education, Research and Practice*. Buckingham: Open University Press.

Falkner, K. P., Levi, L. and Carpenter, T. P. (1999) 'Children's Understanding of Equality: A Foundation for Algebra' in *Teaching Children Mathematics* Vol. 6, No. 4, Dec, pp. 232–36.

Frobisher *et al.* (1999) *Learning to Teach Number*. Cheltenham: Stanley Thornes.

Gray, E. (1997) 'Compressing the Counting Process: Developing a Flexible Interpretation' in I. Thompson (ed.) (1997) *Teaching and Learning Number*. Buckingham: Open University Press.

Haylock, D. (2001) *Mathematics Explained for Primary Teachers*. London: Paul Chapman Publishing.

Hobart, D. (1980) 'Mind Your Language' in *Child Education* Vol. 51, p. 7.

Kane, R. B. (1967) 'The Readability of Mathematical English' in *Journal of Research in Science Teaching* Vol. 5, pp. 296–298.

Mason, J., Burton, L. and Stacey, K. (1985) *Thinking Mathematically*. Harlow: Addison-Wesley Ltd.

Mooney, C. *et al.* (2002) *Primary Mathematics: Teaching Theory and Practice*. Exeter: Learning Matters.

QCA (2000) *Curriculum Guidance for the Foundation Stage*. London: QCA.

Singh, S. (1998) *Fermat's Last Theorem*. London: Fourth Estate.

Straker, A. (1994) *Talking Points in Mathematics*. Cambridge: Cambridge University Press.

Thompson, I. (1994) 'Young Children's Idiosyncratic Written Algorithms for Addition' in *Educational Studies in Maths* Vol. 26, No. 4, pp. 323–45.

Thompson, I. (ed.) (1997) *Teaching and Learning Early Number*. Buckingham: Open University Press.

TTA (2002) *Qualifying to Teach: Professional Standards for the Award of QTS and Requirements for Courses of Initial Teacher Training*. London: TTA.

Achieving QTS

The Achieving QTS series now includes over 20 titles, encompassing *Audit and Test*, *Knowledge and Understanding*, *Teaching Theory and Practice* and *Skills Tests* titles. The series also has two sub-series – the *Reflective Readers* and the *Practical Handbooks*. As well as covering the core primary subject areas, the series addresses issues of teaching and learning, and of theory and practice, across both primary curriculum and secondary phases. You can find more information on each of these titles on our website: www.learningmatters.co.uk

Assessment for Learning and Teaching in Primary Schools
Mary Briggs, Peter Swatton, Cynthia Martin and Angela Woodfield
176pp   ISBN: 1 903300 74 6

Primary English
Audit and Test (second edition)
Doreen Challen
64pp   ISBN: 1 903300 86 X

Primary Mathematics
Audit and Test (second edition)
Claire Mooney and Mike Fletcher
52pp   ISBN: 1 903300 87 8

Primary Science
Audit and Test (second edition)
John Sharp and Jenny Byrne
80pp   ISBN: 1 903300 88 6

Learning and Teaching in Secondary Schools (second edition)
Edited by Viv Ellis
176pp   ISBN: 1 84445 004 X

Passing the ICT Skills Test (second edition)
Clive Ferrigan
80pp   ISBN: 1 84445 028 7

Passing the Literacy Skills Test
Jim Johnson
80pp   ISBN: 1 903300 12 6

Passing the Numeracy Skills Test (third edition)
Mark Patmore
64pp   ISBN: 1 903300 94 0

Primary English: Knowledge and Understanding (second edition)
David Wray, Jane Medwell, George Moore and Vivienne Griffiths
224pp   ISBN: 1 903300 53 3

Primary English: Teaching Theory and Practice (second edition)
David Wray, Jane Medwell, Hilary Minns, Elizabeth Coates and Vivienne Griffiths
192pp   ISBN: 1 903300 54 1

Primary ICT: Knowledge, Understanding and Practice (second edition)
Jane Sharp, Avril Loveless, John Potter and Jonathan Allen
256pp   ISBN: 1 903300 59 2

Primary Mathematics: Knowledge and Understanding (second edition)
Claire Mooney, Lindsey Ferrie, Sue Fox, Alice Hansen and Reg Wrathmell
176pp   ISBN: 1 903300 55 X

Primary Mathematics: Teaching Theory and Practice (second edition)
Claire Mooney, Mike Fletcher, Mary Briggs and Judith McCullouch
192pp   ISBN: 1 903300 56 8

Primary Science: Knowledge and Understanding (second edition)
Rob Johnsey, John Sharp, Graham Peacock and Debbie Wright
232pp   ISBN: 1 903300 57 6

Primary Science: Teaching Theory and Practice (second edition)
John Sharp, Graham Peacock, Rob Johnsey, Shirley Simon and Robin Smith
140pp ISBN: 1 903300 58 4

Professional Studies: Primary Phase (second edition)
Kate Jacques and Rob Hyland
224pp ISBN: 1 903300 60 6

Teaching Arts in Primary Schools
Stephanie Penny, Susan Young, Raywen Ford and Lawry Price
192pp ISBN: 1 903300 35 5

Teaching Citizenship in Primary Schools
Hilary Claire
160pp ISBN: 1 84445 010 4

Teaching Foundation Stage
Edited by Iris Keating
200pp ISBN: 1 903300 33 9

Teaching Humanities in Primary Schools
Pat Hoodless, Sue Bermingham, Elaine McCreery and Paul Bowen
192pp ISBN: 1 903300 36 3

ACHIEVING QTS: REFLECTIVE READERS

Reflective Reader: Primary Professional Studies
Sue Kendall-Seatter
160pp ISBN: 1 84445 033 3

Reflective Reader: Secondary Professional Studies
Simon Hoult
160pp ISBN: 1 84445 034 1

Reflective Reader: Primary English
Andrew Lambirth
128pp ISBN: 1 84445 035 X

Reflective Reader: Primary Mathematics
Louise O'Sullivan, Andrew Harris, Margaret Sangster, Jon Wild, Gina Donaldson and Gill Bottle
128pp ISBN: 1 84445 036 8

Reflective Reader: Primary Science
Judith Roden
128pp ISBN: 1 84445 037 6

Reflective Reader: Primary Special Educational Needs
Sue Soan
128pp ISBN: 1 84445 038 4

ACHIEVING QTS: PRACTICAL HANDBOOKS

Successful Teaching Placement: Primary and Early Years
Jane Medwell
128pp ISBN: 1 903300 92 4

To order please phone our order line 0845 230 9000 or send an official order or cheque to
BEBC, **Albion Close, Parkstone, Poole, BH12 3LL**
Order online at www.learningmatters.co.uk